D0593134

Praise for *Say Anything to Anyone, Anywhere*

"Different is normal serves as a compelling theme throughout this comprehensive look at communication across cultures and its implications for building bridges one to one. Highly informative, entertaining, and readable."

—Dianna Booher, Author of *Communicate with Confidence* and *Creating Personal Presence*

"This book is an essential companion for anyone who works with people from different cultures or travels to different counties. With clear and insightful examples, it shows how to communicate effectively and easily with any culture, anywhere. Well written, educational, and fun! Read before you go."

—Dan Poynter, CSP, Editor of *Global Speakers NewsBrief*

"I can't express how much Gayle's coaching changed my life and career. She has dramatically improved my ability to communicate effectively and speak in public, which has greatly enhanced my effectiveness as a leader. Her methods are now explained in this must-read book."

—Don Finkell, CEO, Shaw Hardwood

"Gayle's approach to presentation coaching has been very beneficial to me. Her techniques, now available in her book, have helped me stand before rooms of hundreds of guests and present with confidence and clarity."

—Key Coker, Dallas City President, BBVA Compass Bank

"I met Gayle when she spoke on effective cross-cultural communication at an Entrepreneurs' Organization (EO) conference in Marrakech. Her book is indispensable to anyone who interacts with different cultures . . . which is everyone!"

—John L. Wade, CEO, Gung-Ho Company

"With the world becoming ever more connected, understanding cultural differences has never been more important to personal and business success. Gayle's book provides a practical and actionable road map for global adventurers to follow."

—**Rich Beck, Senior Vice President,**
PepsiCo Global Operations

"I have worked with Gayle and Circles of Excellence on several occasions over the years in both local and global capacities leveraging their expertise to improve interpersonal communication within my business. This book is the culmination of these perspectives outlining how we can, and need, to adapt to the global culture we live in today."

—**Tim Danks, Executive Director, Assurance and**
Managed Services, Huawei Technologies USA

"Gayle's book gives a unique perspective on the cross-cultural challenges facing today's global business managers. She enlightens us as to the many *visible*, and more often *invisible*, aspects to interactions and communications between team members operating with very different mind-sets and within greatly different paradigms."

—**Mark Dendle, CFO, The ECOM Group**

"Cultural issues in international business are a critical success factor. Few possess the understanding and grasp of the issue better than Gayle. As an international business lawyer, I live her teachings every day."

—**Manuel Rajunov, Partner, Foreign**
Legal Consultant, DLA Piper

"Gayle's seminars and teachings have had great impact on all students, faculty, and administrative staff who had attended our university. I am very pleased to see that Gayle has now brought her expertise to this excellent guide."

—**Rogelio Palomera, Professor, University of**
Puerto Rico at Mayaguez

say anything
to anyone, anywhere

say anything

to anyone, anywhere

5 keys to successful cross-cultural communication

gayle cotton

WILEY

JOHN WILEY & SONS, INC.

Cover image: ma_rish/iStockphoto
Cover design: Wendy Mount

Copyright © 2013 by Circles Of Excellence, Inc. All rights reserved.

Published by John Wiley & Sons, Inc., Hoboken, New Jersey.
Published simultaneously in Canada.

No part of this publication may be reproduced, stored in a retrieval system, or transmitted in any form or by any means, electronic, mechanical, photocopying, recording, scanning, or otherwise, except as permitted under Section 107 or 108 of the 1976 United States Copyright Act, without either the prior written permission of the Publisher, or authorization through payment of the appropriate per-copy fee to the Copyright Clearance Center, 222 Rosewood Drive, Danvers, MA 01923, (978) 750-8400, fax (978) 646-8600, or on the web at www.copyright.com. Requests to the Publisher for permission should be addressed to the Permissions Department, John Wiley & Sons, Inc., 111 River Street, Hoboken, NJ 07030, (201) 748-6011, fax (201) 748-6008, or online at www.wiley.com/go/permissions.

Limit of Liability/Disclaimer of Warranty: While the publisher and author have used their best efforts in preparing this book, they make no representations or warranties with respect to the accuracy or completeness of the contents of this book and specifically disclaim any implied warranties of merchantability or fitness for a particular purpose. No warranty may be created or extended by sales representatives or written sales materials. The advice and strategies contained herein may not be suitable for your situation. You should consult with a professional where appropriate. Neither the publisher nor the author shall be liable for damages arising herefrom.

For general information about our other products and services, please contact our Customer Care Department within the United States at (800) 762-2974, outside the United States at (317) 572-3993 or fax (317) 572-4002.

Wiley publishes in a variety of print and electronic formats and by print-on-demand. Some material included with standard print versions of this book may not be included in e-books or in print-on-demand. If this book refers to media such as a CD or DVD that is not included in the version you purchased, you may download this material at http://booksupport.wiley.com. For more information about Wiley products, visit www.wiley.com.

Library of Congress Cataloging-in-Publication Data:

Cotton, Gayle.
    Say anything to anyone, anywhere : 5 keys to successful cross-cultural communication / Gayle Cotton.
        pages cm
    Includes index.
    ISBN 978-1-118-42042-3 (cloth); 978-1-118-60588-2 (ebk);
    ISBN 978-1-118-60582-0 (ebk); ISBN 978-1-118-60585-1 (ebk)
        1. Intercultural communication. 2. Cultural relations. I. Title.
    HM1211.C68 2013
    303.48'2—dc23

                                                      2012043891

10 9 8 7 6 5 4 3 2 1

Dedicated to my global family of every race and color.
We are all linked by the greatest culture of
all . . . the human culture.

CONTENTS

ACKNOWLEDGMENTS

A heartfelt "Thank you!" to the following people for the roles they played in the writing of this book and for bringing me to this point in my life.

Glenn Doman and the Institutes for the Achievement of Human Potential, for teaching me what amazing things people around the world, both advantaged and disadvantaged, are capable of when given the opportunity.

My dear friends, Paul and Dee Carnes, for showing me how to live my life with faith, passion, and the belief that anything is possible with perseverance.

My friend and "sister," Krystyna Stepien, whose assistance, expertise, and positive outlook were ever present when I began working in Geneva, Switzerland, and around the world.

My parents and wonderful extended family, who taught me that everyone is created equally and deserves the best possible chance to succeed in life.

My three children, who from their moment of birth, showed me that the world of tomorrow will be created by the children of today.

My husband and "pre-editor," whose love and support have been with me throughout the writing of this book.

My Circles Of Excellence team and friends, for their contribution in making this book a success.

My book endorsers, for taking the time out of their busy schedules to read and endorse my book.

Last, but not least, my John Wiley & Sons team, for making this book possible.

INTRODUCTION

Every day, as I take my early morning walk through our neighborhood, I listen to and watch the people familiar to me starting their day. As I walk, I can't help but think about the life that is currently going on in other parts of the world, with different time zones and climates, each place with its own unique approach to the day at that moment in time.

I can see in my mind the bustle of the souks in Dubai. I can hear the sound of Italian men at a corner café saying, "buongiorno!" as others pass by. I can literally taste a fresh-baked pastry from a patisserie in Paris. I can smell the fish being hauled in from the day's catch in bright, colorful nets in Malta, and I can feel the cool breeze as the farmers in the Swiss Alps bring their cows in for the night, bells ringing . . . each with a unique tone of its own.

I'm reminded that life around the world has countless similarities, yet so many differences. How magnificent to imagine this, and how reassuring to know that as I look at the evening stars, children in China are just waking up, families in Australia are preparing their morning breakfast, and the Tokyo subways are a flurry of morning commuter activity.

Our world is a marvelous place now accessible by anyone. What was once so dauntingly large and difficult to explore is now only hours away by plane or a few moments away with real-time technology.

I feel most privileged to have had the opportunity to live and work in different parts of the world. I was prepared for it early on, having been raised by a predominantly Swedish family with a little dash of Irish. My maternal grandmother proudly introduced herself as, "Elsa Astrid Wilhelmina Peterson Nelson!"—stated in the finest Swedish accent. I grew up in a small university town where I was fortunate to interact with people of many nationalities and cultures. I ultimately married a Frenchman who could affectionately be referred to as Pepé Le Pew. Although I never really thought my career would lead me into cross-cultural education on a global basis, it's been a wonderful, delightful, sometimes embarrassing, and certainly a most challenging and rewarding experience.

It all started in 1989, when I moved to Geneva, Switzerland, to work with a corporate training company to develop training programs for international companies and branches of the United Nations. This company eventually led to the creation of Circles Of Excellence Inc.

We developed training programs for marketing, management, and presentation skills, but soon discovered that each and every course needed to be adapted, in some way, for the respective cultures with which we worked. Furthermore, we realized it was necessary to adapt our communication style and presentation approach to even discuss— *let alone sell*—our services! We found we needed to be able to **say anything to anyone, anywhere.** Thus began the **"5 Keys to Successful Cross-Cultural Communication,"** a process we designed for our success as well as for the success of the readers of this book.

5 Keys to Successful Cross-Cultural Communication

Key One—*Create* proactive cross-cultural communication

Key Two—*Rapport* secrets to bridge the cultural gap

Key Three—*Organize* productive interactions

Key Four—*Strategies* for relationships

Key Five—*Success* leaves clues

The first letter of the first word of each key spells the word *cross.* When the first word of each phrase is put together into a phrase, it says the following:

Create Rapport and Organize Strategies for Success

The Cross of Cross-Cultural

This phrase was the key to success for Circles Of Excellence. We discovered that the most important asset in today's easily accessible, global business marketplace was the ability to successfully **cross** from our own **culture** into another. This meant creating common bonds, quality business or social relationships, and ultimately friendships based on respect, trust, and understanding.

As readers will find out, *awareness is the first step . . .*

KEY ONE

Create Proactive Cross-Cultural Communication

Avoid Reactive Communication

The chapters in Key One will cover what you need to know about cultural development in order to be proactive in your cross-cultural communication. Whether you are working with or travelling to different cultures, a pattern in your communication with others is likely to emerge: If you aren't *proactive*, you will be *reactive*. Anyone who has negotiated with different cultures, managed a multicultural workforce, or simply visited other countries knows that first impressions are made quickly—and can last well beyond that initial interaction. It is very difficult to overcome a cultural offense, no matter how unintentional it may be.

We all want to avoid embarrassing miscommunication and misunderstanding. This is why it's so crucial to *proactively* adapt your style and approach in a way that is comfortable for the culture with which you are communicating. You need to understand what makes cultures so different from one another and become aware of what may work against you due to preexisting cultural perceptions.

Cultures are a bit like the chicken and the egg. How did they all begin? Cultural development is influenced by many factors, including language, climate, and environment. These impact the human nervous system, which in turn creates unique variations in communication styles and behavior. As we travel and experience different cultures, these experiences become part of our cultural layers, which in turn makes us more comfortable with cultures other than our own. This basic understanding of cultural science creates the, aha! to enable you to *maximize* effective communication and *minimize* ineffective communication in any culture.

What Makes Cultures So Unique?

Differences Are the Spice of Life!

Have you ever given serious thought to what creates cultural differences? We all know, of course, that these differences *exist*, but what is really involved in making each culture so unique? This is one of the first questions we ask attendees in our cross-cultural classes at Circles Of Excellence. It provokes thought in everyone—and quite the myriad of different responses!

Some people assume we are just born different. Others cite our country, region, and language as forces that create these differences. Then there are those who feel that tradition, beliefs, religion, and family are what make us so distinct from one another. Of course, every one of these answers is absolutely correct; there is no wrong answer.

When we consider the different elements that affect cultural distinctions, we realize that it all starts from our moment of birth. Before we can even see, we hear language all around us—and for the most part, the main language we hear will become our mother tongue language. That language's sounds, expression, and melody will have a profound effect on how we develop and communicate.

As we grow up according to our country's, region's, and even neighborhood's rules and traditions, we develop cultural beliefs and values that will remain with us throughout the rest of our lives. How and where we live creates immediate perceptions about who we are and how we are likely to behave. We're all familiar with the labeling and branding that are implicit in a statement such as, "Oh, you're from *that* neighborhood [or *that* part of town]." It doesn't matter if it's the best or the worst neighborhood or part of town; you've been identified by where you live. Almost everyone who lives in Dallas knows that if you are from Highland Park, you are from one of the oldest, wealthiest neighborhoods, with one of the best *public* school systems in the city. On the other hand, almost everyone is aware of what "being from the wrong side of the tracks" can connote. Of course, our families, friends, teachers, experiences, and religious beliefs reinforce this kind of labeling and branding—and affect our beliefs and values as well. These things ultimately become part of every person's foundation, no matter what culture we claim.

Our gender, race, and ethnic background clearly have a strong impact on our development. How the genders interact and how people from different races or ethnic backgrounds relate to one another play important roles in what we believe is appropriate—or not. Our friends, colleagues, education, and work/life experiences can reinforce these beliefs—and in some cases, dramatically change them.

And let's not forget the impact that different regions or countries to which we travel can have on our approach and outlook. These further define both how we perceive ourselves and how others perceive us. We change dramatically when we travel to places with different cultures and languages from our own. As we absorb these differences and learn to understand or speak another culture's language, it becomes part of who we are. We begin to develop what is referred to as cultural overlay, a blending of our own culture with another. The more we experience other cultures—and especially speak that culture's language—the more cultural overlay and blending we have. For example, as I discussed in the book's Introduction, I was raised by a predominantly Swedish family in the United States and lived in Europe for several years early in my career. I'm now married to a Frenchman and live in the United States. As a result, I've often been asked if I feel more European or American. My answer is that I feel Euro-American, a *blend* of both. I still prefer the long European lunches and the social camaraderie that accompanies them; however, I also like the United States' direct and focused business style.

In addition, the major events that happen in our lives can certainly change our cultural perceptions. Our world, beliefs, values, and how we view life have been forever changed by wars, slavery, the holocaust, tsunamis, earthquakes, famines, and terrorist attacks. And likewise, politics—specifically, different countries' current political regimes and leaders—have a tremendous impact on how we view the nations of our world. When we teach in different countries, natives of those countries have strong feelings about our current president, as well as the United States' recent policies and actions. Indeed, some countries have boycotted the United States for some of our political actions, while others have praised us.

Although we've come a long way—as both a nation and a world—from where we once were, judgment and discrimination still manage to weave their way through the innermost layers of global perception and cultural differences. I often remind myself that if I had been born in a different culture and walked in another's shoes—and had the same experiences as the person in those shoes had—I would likely be quite similar to that person in cultural perspective.

International adoption is a perfect example of this. When a young child of a particular race and ethnic heritage is adopted into a different culture, that child will likely develop the new culture's ethnic preferences, regardless of its native race and heritage. And the younger the child is when adopted, the more likely it is that this will be the case. The older the child is when adopted, the more likely there will be greater native culture retention along with the cultural overlay.

As we begin to truly understand what creates cultural differences, we realize that it's fair to say that "different is normal." Clearly, there is no right or wrong culture; these kinds of distinctions belong to the actions of people within every culture. Even within individual countries, there can be vast cultural distinctions, accents, and languages in different regions. There is no doubt an array of cultural variations within the United States. I have heard many times that the Southern states are "slower and more social" in their business style—a tendency that can be quite annoying to the northeastern states. On the other hand, I've heard that the fast pace of the business style in the northeast can be perceived as "too direct and rude" in the Southern states. And everyone seems to agree that the west coast, especially California, is a "culture unto itself"!

With all our naturally created cultural nuances, distinctions, and unique ways of life, it may come as a surprise that *we do have a culture in common*. This is the human culture, where we share bodies, minds, and hearts in common. This is a culture where we are all created as equals. It's a culture where we live, work, and play on our planet in common . . . Earth. The human culture is where we find our *common bond* and where we are able to connect with one another in mind and spirit. It encompasses each and every one of us, and it can be tapped into at any time and from any place. It is our heritage and the door to understanding both our differences and similarities. It is the *bridge* that we can use to cross from one culture to another.

Understanding the "Cultural Layer Cake"

We All Have Layers in Our Cakes

In this day and age, very few people can claim to be from only one culture. Most of us are like a slice of cultural layer cake, with several cultures blended one on top of the other. In addition to our ancestry, these cultural layers are shaped by a variety of factors. Everything from our race and gender to events and politics contributes to their composition. Anything that has had a strong impact on us, from birth on, is a part of those layers. The influences of our parents, family, friends, neighbors, and teachers have had a hand in creating our cultural makeup.

Think, for example, about a favorite teacher, coach, or boss who may have inspired you in a particular way. Someone like this who had a strong influence on you added to your existing layers—or may have even created a new one.

I remember one university professor in particular who significantly affected my life direction and clearly helped create one of my most important layers. As a typical floundering university freshman, I had no idea what I wanted to do with my life. My SAT scores indicated that I had an aptitude for Russian literature. How that was derived I don't know; however, I do know that it didn't really pique my interest at that point in time!

Everything changed in my second semester, when I took a humanities class from a new professor who forever changed my view of the world. Even after the first class, I knew that humanities and behavioral science would somehow find a place in my career. My professor's point of view about different civilizations around the world, as well as his perspective on global cultures, opened my eyes, and I saw the social and cultural sciences in a whole new light.

He began, interestingly enough, with a foundation in neuroscience, the link of the human culture that connects us all. He then expanded on how neuroscience influences the cultural layers that make each culture so unique. He took us on a journey of exploration that unfolded in an unbiased way, as we experienced cultures from around the world. Ultimately, he challenged us to imagine what our lives would have been like had we been born in a culture other than our own. His advanced classes became so popular that there was a semester's wait to get into them! I'm sure many of the readers of this book have had similar experiences with someone who has had a profound impact on their lives. When this happens, it is difficult to imagine how your life would have turned out had it not been for this person's influence.

As we explore our own and others' cultural layers, we begin to understand how and why we are the way we are. Your parents' and grandparents' ancestry, for instance, directly affect how you are raised to view life and what you consider to be most important. Since I was born into a first-generation Swedish family that had just a touch of Irish from one grandfather, the Swedish culture played an important role in my life. For those who are familiar with the Swedish culture, you're probably aware that they can be a bit more reserved when compared with, for example, the Italian culture (which is an understatement to some!). However, because my grandparents had come to the United States by boat just prior to World War II, they were anxious to learn the English language and adopt the American way of life. They were patriotic and proud to be American, so they experienced cultural overlay very quickly. They rarely spoke in Swedish, and as a result, I really picked up only a few phrases here and there. The only times they *did* speak Swedish were when they didn't want me to know what they were saying! As for my Irish grandfather, he never let the rest of the family forget that he was "the ole Irishman." His influence definitely added some fun and Irish mischief to the family.

When you really look at culture, you recognize that it is a *shared design* for living within family and community. That design influences how we are raised to view and live life. As a result, we begin to develop cultural *tendencies*. Although dominant cultural distinctions affect the culture as a whole, it's important to keep in mind that cultural tendencies develop to varying degrees on an individual basis. As a result, although we need to be aware of the cultural tendencies that may influence a relationship, it's equally important to relate to people as individuals and avoid stereotyping.

Thanks to the ease of travel and today's virtual communication, we are beginning to *homogenize* as a global culture. Some cultural distinctions are blending, and others are disappearing altogether. That was one of the concerns when several countries in Europe formed the European Union (EU). Every country—currently 27—wanted to make sure it retained its own unique language, culture, and way of life. Fortunately (and not surprisingly), each country's unique characteristics have remained intact, and they probably always will.

Today's technology is having a dramatic effect on global cultural homogenization. Almost everyone now has immediate virtual access to other cultures. Consequently, cultural tendencies and distinctions will continue to change as we adopt one another's styles and ways of interacting—and this is how cultural integration and homogenization is happening, in some way, to us all.

The following section provides a list and descriptions for some of the factors that influence how some of our cultural layers originate and affect our behavior.

Some Major Things That Impact Our Cultural Layers

- **Mother tongue and secondary languages**

  Our mother tongue—the first (and sometimes only) language we learn—has one of the strongest influences on our cultural layers. It is the basis for how we initially think, behave, and communicate with one another. Secondary languages usually have a lesser effect, unless that secondary language becomes the predominant language, in which case it could have an equally strong influence.

- **Race**

  The race into which we are born creates a variety of perspectives about our cultural characteristics as well as how others perceive us. We still have a long way to go in eliminating racial prejudice globally; however, as cultures blend and understanding increases, racial inequality is becoming less of a factor in many parts of the world.

- **Ethnicity**

  Ethnicity should not to be confused with race. People can be of a particular race and have different ethnic preferences due to their life experiences and environment. For example, if a Chinese baby is adopted by a non-Chinese family and raised in the United States, the child's race will always be Chinese, but the child's ethnic preferences will most likely be American.

- **Gender**

  Being male or female certainly has an impact on how different countries and cultures view different individuals, as gender equality still varies widely around the world. Even when I first worked in Switzerland in the early 1990s, women didn't have the right to vote in one of their 26 cantons (a canton is similar to a state or province). Fortunately, the need for gender equality is beginning to gain momentum globally, and women around the world are slowly, but surely, cracking that big glass ceiling.

- **Local culture**

  The local culture is the combined influence of your home life, surrounding environment, neighborhood, and city or village. This is where we experience the support system that develops the foundation for our cultural beliefs and values. Much of human behavior is governed by what we value to be the most important to us. Our values influence the standards by which we measure the quality of our lives against those of others. The flavor of our local culture, whether a rice paddy in Asia or a small village in Italy, will clearly influence those standards.

- **Regional attire**

  Attire, and how we are expected to dress, can vary greatly from one culture to the next, as a result of the industry, climate differences, and cultural preferences. In addition, the philosophy regarding what is considered *appropriate* versus *inappropriate* can be very different, and that influences our cultural development and perspective. For example, many Middle Eastern cultures require

Figure 2.1
Business Attire in Dubai

that women cover their heads in public. Some industries, such as banking, require a professional or "buttoned-up" attire, in contrast to other industries where business casual is acceptable. In the UAE, it's not uncommon to see the traditional attire of the Sheikhs along with the standard business attire, as exemplified in the photo in Figure 2.1, which was taken at a conference where I was a speaker.

- **Ancestry**

  Like our mother tongue language, ancestry can have a strong influence on us. This is especially true if we live in the country of our ancestors or if we are first-generation immigrants in another country. This tends to have less influence, respectively, for second- and third-generation immigrants.

- **Parents and family**

  It shouldn't come as a surprise that this is the foundation of our roots and development. Our parents' and family's involvement— or lack of involvement—in our upbringing and lives makes a crucial contribution to our core layers.

- **Teachers**

  Both good and bad teachers strongly affect our cultural layers. Because we spend up to a third of our lives in school—and many people spend even longer than this—their influence helps establish many of our beliefs and values, in addition to guiding our careers and even some personal choices.

- **Friends**

  Friends, colleagues, and peers are also our "teachers." They may, in some cases, even have a stronger influence than our actual teachers. The peer pressure that is often inherent in what our friends feel and say can have a big impact on how we behave and the decisions we make.

- **Our nation or country**

  Certainly our home country, or country of residence, has a profound effect on how we live and what we associate with. Whether we feel a patriotic connection or the desire to live elsewhere, our country—and its corresponding beliefs and values—drives our actions in significant ways.

- **Geographic regions, states, provinces, cantons, etc.**

  It is interesting to note that regions, states, provinces, and cantons within the same country can be vastly different and possibly have an even greater influence on our cultural layers than our country of residence. The cantons in Switzerland that speak German, French, Italian, and Romansh (the fourth national language of Switzerland) are a perfect example of this. The Swiss Germans in Zurich tend to be more reserved in their social and business style in comparison to the Swiss French in Geneva, whereas both the Swiss Germans and the Swiss French are more reserved and less expressive than the Swiss Italians in Lugano.

- **Cities, towns, and villages**

  Like regions of a country, cities, towns, and villages have very distinct characteristics that can have a dramatic influence on how we view life. The difference between living in a large city and a small town or village will certainly create unique cultural layers. Life will be quite different for a child growing up in New York City compared with a child growing up in a remote African village. Whereas the child in New York expects to deal with cars and traffic, the child in the African village more likely expects to deal with wild animals and potential dangers.

- **Neighborhoods**

  Neighborhoods influence and define us within the context of our city, town, or village. They can imply status, wealth, poverty, a specific ethnicity, or simply a unique section of town. We all know of neighborhoods that create certain perceptions about the people who live in them.

- **Border countries, states, and provinces**

  Border countries definitely have an influence on our cultural layers, and this is especially the case in smaller countries with easy access to other countries, such as those in Europe. Even a country as large as the United States—with Canada to the north and Mexico to the south—can count on these two nations to have a major impact on U.S. culture in states near those borders.

- **Religion**

  Religion is often one of the dominant or core layers in our development, and it is one that can be directly connected to an entire culture's history. It is frequently the judgment factor between different cultures. It creates tremendous passion in people and consequently has been the cause of many wars.

- **Social class**

  Social class, in varying degrees, is apparent in every country and culture around the world. There are the wealthy and the middle class in the United States, the dukes and duchesses in England, and the counts and countesses in France, along with all the other levels of global nobility and royalty. In many cases, one's social class is designated by birth and remains with the person throughout his or her life. I'll always remember the time my daughter was hospitalized in France. She had a private room with her first and last name on the door. In contrast, all the room doors around her had the titles of counts and countesses or other noble designations. It was rather humorous, because her door was the one that everyone noticed because she had no title!

- **Education**

  The level of our education and our vocations of choice greatly influence our view of life. They often supersede old cultural layers that we've outgrown or that have changed as a result of our experience. A good example is the technical industry, which is now led by people from India, China, and many other parts of the world. Due to the possibilities that were available to highly trained technical engineers, it has become a field of choice that has opened doors for them to be able to live and work all over the world.

- **Profession**

  Our choice of profession, where we work, and what type of companies we work for is clearly a chief component of our lives—because this is where more than half of our life learning and growth happens. It is the place where we spend all day, every day, and therefore makes a huge contribution to the development of our cultural layers.

- **Workplace colleagues**

  The people with whom we work—as well as their views, habits, and attitudes—have a substantial effect on how we perceive our work environment and fellow colleagues. Today's international workplace is very multicultural, so lots of learning goes on both interpersonally and virtually. The experiences we have working with colleagues in our own country or abroad will definitely add to our layers.

- **Experiences**

  These are what change our existing layers and perspective. Life experiences alter and expand the way we view people, cultures, and countries and what we consider to be comfortable (and uncomfortable). For example, after I worked in Asia for a period of time, it became very comfortable for me to bow slightly while making a two-handed business card exchange. I actually become so comfortable with this practice that I found myself doing the same after returning home to the United States, even with credit cards! And while living in Geneva, I always asked the bank tellers if they spoke English, so it was pretty surprising to a teller in the United States when I asked the same thing in French!

- **Events**

  You may wonder how events influence our cultural layers. Yet events are one of the major things that affect how different cultures interact and feel about one another. They can change our cultural perspectives overnight. American companies were boycotted in some places when the United States bombed Iraq without getting support from the United Nations, France, and certain other European countries. In the United States, "French fries" became "freedom fries," French wine sales dropped, and U.S. citizens avoided French restaurants. On the other hand, when the United States killed Osama bin Laden, Americans were touted as heroes. Events can play a strong role on how cultures perceive one another.

- **Politics**

   Like events, politics and world leaders have a strong impact on the global perspective of different countries. Leaders, and the decisions they make, can sometimes be beloved and hated simultaneously depending on where you are and whom you are talking to. The "Shock and Awe" of the Iraq War was both cheered in the United States and booed in many other parts of the world. These mixed feelings were evident everywhere I traveled during that time.

- **Travel**

   Travel, undoubtedly, has a tremendous effect on how we feel about other cultures. When you visit a country, you can see and learn firsthand about a culture. More often than not, we are surprised by the similarities and things we have in common, rather than being judgmental about the differences. It can be a real eye-opener, and we usually get a glimpse of the human compassion present in every culture. Virtual travel also expands our cultural layers and helps us learn more about other cultures.

- **Physically challenged**

   This is definitely something that cannot be ignored when you discuss cultural layers. The experiences of those with physical challenges and those who interact with the physically challenged unquestionably impact our thoughts, feelings, and how we relate to one another—no matter what culture we are from. This was apparent to anyone who saw the 2012 Paralympics. The triumphs of the physically challenged are triumphs for the entire human culture.

As we explore what creates our unique cultural layers, we begin to recognize that even those who claim to be of *one* specific race or ethnicity still experience many things—and have many qualities—that affect their layers. And when we observe how different elements of life affect these layers, we can better understand the cultural overlay we *all* have. Everyone's layers were initially created and were then overlaid with new and possibly very different layers of information. Cultural overlay puts a fresh perspective on our existing layers and can even *completely* change the nature of our core layers.

Exposure to different life settings is a good example of how cultural overlay happens. Let's say that you've always lived in a rural setting; you probably have a layer of what *security* means based on that environment. Moving to a big city would then add to that layer by giving you an expanded view of what *security* means in a city environment. This new experience has altered your original core layer and your notion of security. The same thing happens in a broader sense when we travel from one country to another. We experience new languages, different ways of communicating, and more current perceptions of what is considered appropriate or inappropriate in that country's context. Our original layers of understanding change and expand our core layer to include another country's culture.

One of my most memorable business examples of cultural overlay was when I met a Swedish customer for the first time, right in my own city of Dallas. Since he had recently arrived from Sweden, I expected him to have a typically more reserved Swedish manner. To the contrary, he greeted me in a cowboy hat, gave me a good firm "Texas handshake," and proceeded to enthusiastically talk about the type of cultural training his company needed. After I recovered from my surprise, I started thinking about his cultural overlay. I asked him where he had lived *besides* Sweden. He told me that he had managed the company operations for the past several years in Italy. He said that the differences between the Swedish and Italian cultures had given him the ability to be comfortable with most any culture and that now he was trying to be Texan! It was obvious that his Italian overlay had dramatically influenced his core Swedish style. He went on to tell me that although his Swedish colleague, whom we were subsequently going to meet, had been in the United States for 12 years, he still took a very "Swedish" approach. In other words, this colleague preferred and was still more comfortable with a reserved style. Consequently, when we met his colleague, we both adapted our communication style accordingly.

A more personal example of cultural overlay occurred when I moved to Geneva, Switzerland, and my daughter arrived after me. She stepped off the plane and was in anguish within 30 minutes. She couldn't understand or read the language, and she thought all the buildings were "old and ugly." She wondered why there were "no shiny, new buildings like in Dallas." Her whole world had changed. It was a year before she learned to appreciate the classic architecture and the French language (in which she subsequently became nearly fluent). At that point, her core layer of life in Dallas had changed and expanded to include Geneva and the European way of life.

The next time you meet someone from another culture, or meet someone who is quite different from what you expect, think about what might comprise his or her cultural layers. Ask some general questions about the other person's experiences and share some things about yours. This kind of interaction could be your key to understanding each other. And above all, keep in mind that cultural tendencies are just tendencies. We all have layers in our cake, and those layers are the *link* to our multicultural understanding.

CHAPTER

3

How Many Strikes Are Against You?

Managing Preexisting Cultural Perceptions and Misconceptions

Every country's citizens have to deal with other countries' and cultures' preexisting cultural perceptions or "strikes" against us. And we all have preconceived notions about countries and cultures other than our own.

If we happen to be a "U.S. American," we've probably heard comments about "dumb Americans" based on another culture's perceptions of our ignorance of other countries, their languages, their ways of life, and even geography. One of the things I often hear from other cultures is that many U.S. Americans don't know their geography as well as they should. (I think most of us *would* admit that many U.S. Americans could use a good world geography lesson!) Roper Public Affairs conducted several surveys for the National Geographic Society that concluded that the average U.S. American aged 18 to 24 answered *incorrectly* 50 to 70 percent of the time when asked to locate various countries around the world. The Association of American Geographers in Washington, DC, called the results "alarming and discouraging." I refer to Americans from the United States as U.S. Americans because when you think about it, there are North Americans, South Americans, Central Americans, and Latin Americans, so who are the *real* Americans? Technically, all the countries that are part of the North American Free Trade Agreement (NAFTA), which includes the United States, Canada, and Mexico, or the Central American Free Trade Agreement (CAFTA), which includes Costa Rica, the Dominican Republic, El Salvador, Guatemala, Honduras, Nicaragua, and the United States, can claim to be American. As a result the term *American* has taken on broader meaning in many senses, so some countries have started using the term U.S. American. Unfortunately, this is sometimes shortened to the term *U.S.ers*, which doesn't have the best connotation when you look at how it's spelled. In light of that, *U.S. American* seems to be the term of preference.

When I started working in Switzerland in the early 1990s, I taught communication, management, and sales courses based on behavioral and cultural science. I was working at United Nations branches in Geneva, as well as for many international companies around Europe and Africa. It didn't take long for me to find out that I already had three strikes against me—strikes that definitely affected my credibility. In fact, with a group of senior bankers in Zurich, you would have thought I was from Mars or wearing a rainbow-colored wig given how surprised they were when they realized I was their instructor!

I now often ask my current audience members to guess what those three strikes against me were. Most of them are pretty quick to respond with the fact that I am American. Strike 1—since the European perception is generally something like, "What do Americans know about different cultures?"

Next, someone in the audience will usually identify strike 2: the fact that I am female. At that time, in the early 1990s, it was less common for a woman to be teaching at that level of expertise. In fact, when I first worked in Europe, it was more than a year before I even had a woman *attend* one of my classes. Many working women simply weren't in a high enough position to need this type of training.

My third strike is a bit more difficult to guess. It takes audiences longer to come up with this one, or perhaps they are afraid to say it! I typically have to nudge them by referring to my appearance. At that point, someone will usually yell out with the obvious fact that I am blonde. Strike 3! I found out that, unfortunately, all those dumb blonde jokes are a global phenomenon.

And in my case, it didn't even stop at three strikes. I had a few others against me, and many had to do with appearance. Being short seemed to affect my credibility, so I started wearing very high heels—and I haven't stopped since. And although pants suits were perfectly acceptable for women in the United States, skirts were preferred in Europe. In regard to color choices, the old IBM dress code of suits in black, dark blue, gray, brown, or possibly cream in warmer months were the best choices. For a more professional look, I gave up the currently fashionable big hair of the nineties that I had brought from Dallas and put my blonde locks up in a more conservative French twist. To add a bit of sophistication, I even wore a pair of nonprescription glasses. Soon the updated appearance was dubbed my *librarian look*. But whatever you call it, it seemed to work; I felt like these members of the European business world were beginning to take me more seriously.

But my looks weren't the only thing I needed to alter to be successful with the various cultures of Europe and Africa. I also needed to make some actual changes in my professional approach. I found it was necessary to modify my communication and presentation for a more serious and low-key style. For example, training in the United States is commonly dubbed enter*train*ment. That is, we tend to *entertain* as we *train*, and our audience members both expect and appreciate this. We interact with the audience, smile a lot, add a bit of humor, and inject some fun.

However, at this time in Europe—and in many other parts of the world—a more educational or professor style was better received. I would start my presentations on a serious, professional, and almost stern note. I stood very tall and barely cracked a smile for the first hour. I used facts and figures early on to establish credibility. As the audience warmed up to me and I gained their respect, I slowly added some elements of enter*train*ment. Changing my approach definitely helped me overcome the strikes and preexisting cultural perceptions working against me. This change in speaking and presentation style is still necessary in some parts of the world and with certain audiences. However, global audiences are changing as cultures homogenize. I now coach many speakers, trainers, and presenters from around the world on the art of enter*train*ment—and some of my most frequent customers nowadays are from Europe!

There are innumerable *stereotypical* preconceived notions and cultural perceptions. Anyone who has visited Paris has probably heard that "Parisians are rude." We've been told, "Everything in Italy is always on strike." Who hasn't heard, "Customer service representatives in India and other countries aren't helpful"? After the cold war, many people thought that "Russians were cold and unfriendly." World War II left cultural perceptions about Germany and Japan that have taken decades to overcome. Today, the perception of both Germany and Japan is more apt to be "masters in technology and engineering."

Preexisting cultural perceptions also go beyond specific countries and cultures and exist *within* the countries themselves. In fact, these are frequently the cause of contention and wars in those countries. Look at North and South Vietnam, North and South Korea, and the Northern and Southern United States during the Civil War. And these cultural perceptions within countries don't die easily. Someone from the southern United States referred to me as a Yankee not too long ago, even though I'm from Washington State, not Washington, DC!

The question then becomes: How do we overcome or get past these cultural perceptions? How much do you need to compensate, or adapt, for the strikes against you? The answer is simple: You do as much as you feel comfortable doing to achieve the results you want. Some people choose to adapt as little as possible, which often steers them toward a career or profession where less adaptation is necessary—and this, of course, is perfectly acceptable. Although most people are comfortable adapting to a certain extent, others may feel that this could be perceived as inauthentic, or they don't want to put forth the effort to learn that much about another culture. It all depends on what you are comfortable with.

On the other hand, some people choose to travel and interact with different cultures on a regular basis. This usually allows them to become very proficient at adjusting their communication style and approach and helps them create comfortable relationships with people from various cultures around the world. Most of us tend to adapt to a certain extent, whether we are consciously aware of it or not. Doing so creates a comfort zone that makes our cross-cultural interactions easier.

However, there are times when adapting can be uncomfortable—and we therefore need to decide whether we want to do it or not. For example, most professional salespeople are initially very uncomfortable with the long periods of silence that occur during negotiations in many parts of Asia. Consequently, they often speak too soon and end up giving away too much or conceding too early in the process. They learn these lessons the hard way. Usually, salespeople who continually work with Asian customers and clients eventually become comfortable with the silence and long pauses. It becomes one of their cultural layers.

Attire protocol can also be unfitting at times. I remember the first time I presented in Jeddah, Saudi Arabia, in 1998. There were many things, including attire and the expectations of women, that I found rather uncomfortable. However, I abided by the protocol by covering my head and body with the appropriate attire, and I was willing to comply to achieve what I was there for. In doing so, I gained valuable experience and empathy for women, both of which definitely added to my cultural layers in a positive way.

That being said, cultural protocol can quickly change. When I first presented in Dubai, UAE, in 1998, it was recommended for women to wear long sleeved blouses and longer skirts (no minis) or pants. Covering your head was, and still is, optional. However, when I returned a couple of years ago, I saw women wearing mini-skirts and sleeveless blouses and tank tops!

The important thing is to know about the typical preexisting cultural perceptions that *likely* exist in a particular country or culture about *your* country or culture. Keep in mind that these perceptions are just *possible* tendencies; as cultures homogenize, tendencies can change or disappear altogether.

Next, look at your personal characteristics. Are you extremely tall and going to a culture where people are typically shorter in stature? If so, you may want to assume a more relaxed, but not slouching, posture. There is no need to draw more attention to your height by throwing your shoulders back and standing as tall as you possibly can. This might be intimidating to your shorter counterparts. On the other hand, if you are short and are with taller people, stand as tall as you possibly can with your best posture (and if you're a woman—take a page from my book and get some heels!).

Gender issues can also be unnerving. Are you a female who will be working with a predominantly male business culture in another country? In that case, it may be best to have a male counterpart accompany you. Although this may seem sexist and not sit well with many women, sometimes to accomplish the business at hand, we need to put our own feelings aside and do what is best to accomplish the desired outcome. We once had a customer that was working on a very large consulting contract in China. They lost it because they sent a *lone* female to negotiate with a team from the Chinese company—and it did not go over well at all. The Chinese typically negotiate as a team, and consequently, they expect more than just one person to be sent to negotiate with them.

Negotiations usually happen at the senior level, and since there are typically more men at that level in China, they tend to expect a man to be part of the counter negotiating team. Whether you're travelling for business or pleasure, it is wise to adapt accordingly if there are obvious cultural differences regarding communication, attire, protocol, and etiquette.

Overcoming your "strikes"—whether just one or two or many—and preexisting cultural perceptions is most often a matter of using common sense and getting some education. If adapting to a particular culture or country is truly beyond your personal comfort zone, it's probably best that you don't work with or travel to that culture or country. It's good to push our boundaries a bit; however, you don't want to do so to the extent that it is truly uncomfortable for you. If we are out of integrity with ourselves, other cultures will pick up on that immediately. We won't be congruent, and that will work against everyone who is involved—and everything they're trying to accomplish.

Awareness is the first step when you're trying to offset the strikes against you. The next step is to adapt in ways that are comfortable, but not necessarily natural, for you. And don't be surprised when the culture you are interacting with adapts to you first, and you don't need to do anything at all!

CHAPTER

4

Cultural Science

How Neurological Development Affects Cultures

Cultural science is at the very heart of understanding *how* and *why* cultures develop as they do. It *bridges the gap* in our cultural awareness and helps remove the veil of judgment that exists between cultures. It sheds a light on cross-cultural communication and proactive interactions. Exploring cultural science opens up a whole new world of possibilities relating to proactive cultural interactions.

It's probably not surprising that neurological development is the backbone of cultural science. I know—this sounds complicated and complex. And it *can* be when you analyze the environmental and economic factors of entire civilizations. However, from the perspective of understanding cross-cultural communication styles, it is really very logical, easy to understand, and *uncomplicated*. Akin to behavioral science—which focuses on behavior development—cultural science focuses on how our cultural development affects our behavior and our social styles (the individual patterns and behavioral characteristics exhibited in interpersonal communication). It explores how various environment factors and cultural distinctions affect our neurological development through our five senses.

Countless variables come into play for people who are born in different parts of the world. Everything we are exposed to from the moment of birth leaves an imprint on our brains, which, in turn, affects our neurological patterns. The *variety* of different cultural experiences and stimulation received is directly connected to our neurological and behavioral development.

The five senses—visual, auditory, kinesthetic (touch, feeling, and emotion), smell, and taste—have the task of receiving information from our cultural experiences. Is our environment hot or cold? Are we wearing heavy or light clothes? What sounds are surrounding us? Are they loud or soft, familiar or threatening? What does the language others are speaking sound like? What are we seeing visually? Is the environment bright or dark? Is there lots of sun or very little? What tactile sensations do you feel? Are they warm and comfortable or cold and hard? What about smells? Are they pleasant or pungent? What does the food you're eating taste like? Taste has an obvious impact on cultural preferences. What may be a delicacy in one culture could be rather disgusting in another! I've been offered shark fin soup, dog, horse, blowfish, camel sticks, frog legs, tripe (French pig intestines in a sauce similar to chitlins in the southern United States), and chocolate-covered everything, from ants to grasshoppers. What is considered familiar and delicious is all a matter of taste!

The nervous system sends signals through the five senses faster than any technology we have can measure. These signals imprint the brain and eventually turn into *patterns* that affect behavior. These developing patterns can differ *vastly* for children from different continents, countries, cities, and even families. Cultural familiarity creates "comfort zones" that are unique in custom and tradition. The comfort zones of a child growing up in Ketchikan, Alaska, will certainly differ from those of a child growing up in Kenya, and both will differ from those of a child who grows up in New York City. Each child's brain patterns, nervous system, cultural preferences, and behavior take form in a unique and individual way. How each child relates to security, community, and responsibility will be specific to the needs of their environments and will thus create behavior to allow survival within those environments.

Cross-cultural communication distinctions are one of the major things that cultural science has helped identify—and environmental factors play a big role. For example, people who live in a colder climate and wear layers of warm clothes have a tendency to talk with purpose, have less expressive tonality, and minimize body language. If we think about this, it makes perfect sense. Consider how cultures with colder climates developed; there weren't modern methods of heat. Being cold was a part of the lifestyle. Unless you were sitting in front of a warm fire, you didn't have long, drawn-out communication; conversations were more brief and to the point. As a result, tonality was less important, and the constraints of warm, heavy clothing inhibited body language. Getting to the point of the discussion, and moving on, was the goal. Social conversation and small talk became a warm luxury with friends and family.

Climate also has an impact on the development of a culture's mother tongue language. The languages that developed in colder climates have fewer words ending with vowels. The words are apt to be more precise and have fewer multiple meanings or nuances. Due to the precise quality of the language, the total number of words in the language is typically less. Various resources cite that the Germanic languages—which are quite precise and developed in colder climates—have 150,000 to 300,000 words, which seems very approximate. On the other hand, the Latin-based languages—which developed in warmer climates and are known for having many nuances—could have up to 500,000 or more words. Although no one really knows the exact number of words in a particular language, it's interesting to note the differences in communication styles that exist within these two different language cultures.

Brain patterns favor more direct communication in colder climates, with less tonal variation and demonstrative body language. Part of this is because languages ending in consonants, rather than vowels, have less melody to them; and the less melodic the language, the less tonality and body language people use. As a result, individuals from these cultures don't really learn how to use more demonstrative tonality and body language in communication. And if you're not familiar with how it feels to express yourself in these ways, it's awkward when you first try doing it. In addition, you are likely to be less comfortable with people who do use more expressive tonality and body language.

Tonality and body language also impact our facial expressions. It's no secret that photos of people from colder climates show them looking more serious, with fewer smiles than photos of people from warmer cultures. Think of photos you may have seen of Eskimos in the arctic, or the Russians in the streets of Moscow on a cold winter day, compared with photos you have seen of people vacationing in the tropics!

In contrast, languages in warmer climates tend to have more words ending with vowels. A vowel at the end of a word gives a lift or a double vowel sound to the word. Vowels connect the words into song-like phrase, which creates more language melody—something we notice with warm climate dialects and accents as well. The U.S. Southern accent is a good example of this, as Southerners have actually romanticized the English language. The phrase "You all come on over to my house for a barbecue tonight" sounds more like, "Y'alle come on over to mya house for a barbecuea tonitea" when someone from the South says it.

From a neurological perspective, tonality and body language correspond to, and move with, the melody of the spoken language. The more melodic a language is, the more expressive and varied the tone of voice and body language will be. Consequently, the communication styles in warmer climates will usually have more demonstrative or animated tonality and body language.

The choice of words in warm weather cultures is also typically more expressive. Words may have multiple meanings and nuances. There is more social conversation and small talk. Whereas someone from Finland will tend to be more direct and to the point in his or her business communication, someone from Spain will be more apt to ask how you are, discuss something more casually to start, and use more expressive body language to accompany the conversation. People in warmer climates wear lighter clothes, which gives freedom of body movement and allows more body language. Because warm weather cultures have less constraint from cold weather elements, conversation is more relaxed. It may not be as direct, to the point, and purpose-driven as it is in colder climates.

Warmer climate languages—especially those that speak the romantic or Latin-based languages, such as Italy, Spain, or Brazil, to name a few—usually include more words than the colder climate languages. The cultures that use these warmer climate languages take great joy in elaborate, eloquent conversations full of adjectives, adverbs, and nuances. They are interested in a word's context and nuances and love to explore subjects in depth. Debating the pros and cons and negotiating can be an art. In many of the marketplaces of warmer climate cultures such as Spain, India, Egypt, Morocco, or the UAE, bargaining, bartering, and negotiating are as important as the actual purchase itself. I've come home with leather goods, jewelry, shoes, art, and carpets that were not only a good buy but had a story behind them as well!

Cultural studies have shown that many other environmental factors play a big role in cross-cultural behavior and communication styles.

For example, living in a big, fast-paced city such as Tokyo, Delhi, Paris, Hong Kong, or New York City seems to have a similar effect as living in colder climates. Because of these cities' high-speed way of life, there is less social conversation or small talk, tonality is typically less expressive, and body language seems more limited. The pace of communication is quicker, more direct, and to the point. The choice of words, no matter what language is spoken, tends to be more precise and focused.

On the other hand, smaller towns or villages that operate at a slower pace tend to have more relaxed and leisurely communication styles. People who live in these areas engage in more social conversation and small talk. Tonality becomes more expressive, and body language becomes more demonstrative.

Cultural science explores all the elements involved in civilization creation. It analyzes specific cultures' impact on neurological, behavioral, and social development. It gives us clues to language development based on environmental factors and bridges the cultural gap with understanding and awareness. Ultimately, it enables us to proactively communicate and adapt to the different styles of various cultures. It is a fascinating science and has opened many doors in cross-cultural education.

CHAPTER

5

The Chicken or the Egg of Culture

Which Came First? Climate and Environment or Language and Behavior?

Culture is a bit like the chicken and the egg scenario in that no one really knows what came first in cultural development. Cultural science looks at how mother tongue languages, different climates, and environmental factors affect communication and behavioral styles. The big question is: Did mother tongue languages develop *because* of the climate and environmental factors, or did the cultures that spoke a particular language *settle in* climates and environments that best suited their communication and behavior styles? This is truly a fascinating topic to ponder, especially when you consider the multitude of languages, alphabets, symbols, and hieroglyphs around the world.

Fascinating though it may be, when it comes down to it, it really doesn't matter. What *does* matter is that we develop a basic understanding of how and why cultures became what they are today. We can accept what we understand, but it's difficult to accept what we don't. All too often, we've heard attendees in our cross-cultural courses say they had

31

simply been told, "Do this or that," for various cultures. They had no understanding of *why* they were supposed to do this or that, which made it a challenge for them to remember and act on. For example, if you don't understand the purpose of the long pauses and silence in conversations in Asia, you will tend to act instinctively and quickly say something to interrupt the silence. It's difficult to connect the dots if you don't know why you're doing it. Attending our cross-cultural courses led to an aha! moment of awareness for them. It all made sense, and they finally "got it." Once they were aware of the logical reasons that supported what they had learned, it became much easier for them to remember and implement their behavior. Furthermore, they could logically anticipate possible differences in cultures that we may not have specifically addressed in the course.

Proactive preparation based on awareness is the first step in successful cross-cultural interactions. Whether it's for business or pleasure, the idea behind this is to step into another culture's shoes for a moment and then anticipate people's actions and responses. If you can develop an understanding of the culture—and therefore determine which behaviors and methods of communication you can likely expect—it's easier to be more congruent while you're adapting as you may need to. After all, if you lived in the same environment and spoke the same language, you would likely have similar behavior and communication styles. When you don't judge whether a particular style is "right or wrong"—and instead simply adapt to it for the purpose of having a comfortable, productive interaction—you can be true to yourself and the person or persons with whom you are interacting. This kind of congruency leads to credibility, and credibility leads to trust and a comfort zone between the parties involved.

Some people wonder how far you should attempt to adapt to achieve a comfort zone. As we stated in the previous chapter, adapt as much as is comfortable for you. There is nothing worse than having someone perceive you as insincere or lacking congruency because you yourself don't believe in what you are doing. By understanding something about cultural development and putting yourself in the shoes of others in that culture, you will come across as sincere and credible.

Who is responsible for being proactive and adapting first in cross-cultural relationships? This is another chicken and egg scenario for which there is no single correct answer. Whoever is proactively prepared to adapt to the behavior and communication styles of another culture should do it. This is especially important when meeting for the first time. Ideally, both parties should adapt to a certain extent, because this shows each side's willingness to adjust to different ways of doing things. As cultures are exposed to each other more frequently, people will (and should) adapt more often, allowing communication to meet somewhere in the middle.

There is something to be said about the adage "When in Rome, do as the Romans." Cultural etiquette would dictate that we do just that. Adapting to the culture of the country you are visiting is certainly the polite thing to do. In some ways, we Americans are lucky; because English is known as the international language, the expectation that most people will speak some English in other countries already exists. However, native English speakers can't say the same about their ability in the respective country's language. If you can speak some of the native language for the countries you visit, by all means, *do so*. No matter how poorly you speak or how bad your accent is, people will appreciate it. Even simply learning a few basic words before you visit a country can make a big difference in perception. My French husband doesn't accept my "Genevoise" dialect (similar to the Québécois or Cajun French dialects) as *real* French; however, he certainly appreciates the fact that I have some ability to speak his language. No one expects you to speak a second language perfectly. When my husband speaks English, he certainly has an accent. He has caused many chuckles talking about his trips to "Misery" (Missouri) and "our Kansas" (Arkansas). The point is that no one really cares what you sound like; they care that *you* care enough to try to speak their language.

Your profession also can dictate who should adapt first in cross-cultural relationships. If you are in sales and have a client coming to your country for a meeting, it's a nice gesture to show that you know something about his or her country in terms of greetings, dining, and gifts, among other things. If a salesperson has customers visiting the United States from Japan, it's important to see that they are entertained, shown the sights, and taken care of because that is what they would do if you were visiting Japan. Leaving them to their own navigation, as is common to do in the United States, would be considered impolite. This goes a long way toward making your guest feel welcome and comfortable, because it conveys that the other person's culture is important to you—even though that person is in *your* country. At that point, your guests will likely be prepared to conduct business and socially participate in your country's customary ways.

We need to realize that clients or customers who visit our country may still come with some of their own customs. For instance, I have a U.S. client that was expecting Korean customers to visit. His guests came with beautiful gifts for my client and his entire team. My client had not thought about giving or receiving gifts. How sad and embarrassing it was for him, and his team, when they greeted their guests empty handed. Unfortunately, he had not consulted with me beforehand, or I certainly would have prepared him for the gift giving. Although gift giving isn't important in all cultures, it is very important in some, especially the Asian cultures. It's difficult to know for sure what to expect with multicultural guests, so it's best to be discreetly prepared for likely possible scenarios. This also applies when we are the business guests in another country.

Management is another profession the may require some multicultural adapting. When your staff know that you know something about their culture and how they prefer to do things, it fosters cooperation, trust, and respect. After all, people are more apt to do their best work for managers they like, feel comfortable with, and know care about them.

For those with the knowledge and awareness, intuition is often the best guide. However, there are no hard-and-fast rules, so if you sense someone is uncomfortable or confused, adapt and see what happens. You can identify how others interpret the meaning of your communication or action by the response you get, so let that response be your guide. If it isn't what you wanted or expected, chances are, you may be miscommunicating in words or actions according to the cultural interpretation.

Because cultural distinctions are just tendencies, the best we can do is be proactively aware and prepared. This is clearly better than being unprepared and finding ourselves in a reactive cycle or creating misunderstanding.

There is a chicken and egg theory behind every culture. At the very least, simply by knowing the culture's location, something about its environment, and what languages are spoken, you can draw some rational and reasonable conclusions about how to proactively prepare.

Maximize Effective Communication

... By Minimizing Ineffective Communication

Listening is one of the first and most important things we need to keep in mind when communicating cross-culturally. Because of unfamiliar accents, inaccuracies, and possibly a limited ability in a second language, to make sure we've understood correctly, we need to listen even *more* carefully than we might when communicating in our native tongue. We have two ears and one mouth for a reason!

For the most part, people are rather poor listeners, with the exception of people from Asian cultures and a few others. People from these cultures typically listen quite carefully. They usually politely pause and contemplate what has been said before they respond. Sometimes there are even long periods of silence before they respond. Although this can be uncomfortable to some people, it would benefit many of us to listen more carefully and to contemplate our responses more than we do. Because we spend so much of our time preparing what we will say next, we consequently miss a big part of what someone else has said. We may then say something that isn't relevant, doesn't make sense, or shows the other person that we didn't listen. Sound familiar? Rather than listening for the real meaning of what someone is saying, we are often distracted by accents, mispronunciation, grammar, or a simplified level of speech.

For instance, I was recently at a hotel in Africa where the clerk was talking to me about a "wee fee." It was several minutes before I realized he meant Wi-Fi. Most people tend to listen only for the facts and not the *underlying meaning*, which is so important in multicultural communication. We become impatient, make hasty judgments, and don't confirm what we've understood—something that's especially crucial to do when communicating with people from other cultures. Being a good listener goes a long way in maximizing effective communication and minimizing ineffective communication.

Whether you are working with people from different cultures or traveling to different cultures, if you aren't proactive in your communication, you will likely be reactive. There are really only two types of communication: effective communication and miscommunication. So if you didn't communicate effectively, you have probably miscommunicated in some way. Anyone who has negotiated with people from different cultures, managed a multicultural workforce, or simply visited other countries has probably experienced this. It's very difficult to get out of the reactive cycle of miscommunication once you get yourself into one—no matter how unintentional it may have been.

Avoiding miscommunication and misunderstanding is essential to successful cross-cultural relationships. This requires you to *proactively* adapt your approach in a way that works for another culture. Chances are, others will likely do the same with you, thereby allowing both parties to establish a comfortable middle ground. Several years ago, I was visiting a friend in Geneva while her Polish mother was there. Her mother didn't speak any English, and I certainly didn't speak any Polish. We both spoke some French; however, our French was rather limited at that time. There were many French words we didn't know, especially for objects or nouns. We also didn't have smartphones with instant translation ability back then, and the dictionary took too long. So we simply created our own words. It was easier than inserting a Polish or English word that one or the other of us would have to learn and remember. If we agreed that a plate would be called an "oodo," then an "oodo" it was. To this day, when I see my friend's mother, we sometimes fall back on our unique version of French—while her daughter and family simply smile and shake their heads.

Much like this situation, there are some scenarios that require us to be proactive in ways that we may not have imagined. I had gotten married the year before we incorporated Circles Of Excellence in Dallas, and my name was now Gayle Cotton-Delpierre. Although Gayle Cotton was the business name I had used in Europe, I decided to use my full married name in Dallas. I had no idea what I was in for with that decision! I have to admit, Delpierre can be a bit difficult to pronounce correctly. I just can't seem to get that French "r" in *Delpierrrre* to sound the way the French say it.

Well, if I thought *I* had a problem, the Texans certainly didn't do much better. I was called Gayle Cotton-Delper, Gayle Cotton-Delpree, Gayle Cotton-Delpierreee, but when it got to Gayle Cotton-Del Prairie I knew something had to change. I may joke about moving from the land of Swiss cows to the land of Texas cows, but I wasn't about to be dubbed Gayle Cotton Del Prairie! So I made the proactive decision to drop Delpierre from my business name. It was a smart decision, because I soon realized that Cotton really was a good business name for Texas, especially with the Cotton Bowl in Dallas. I'm sure some of my readers have made similar decisions to further their career in different parts of the United States or other countries. I know many people from China, who are now living and working in the United States, who have adopted Western names such as Henry or Betty for the same reason I did—pronunciation!

Maximizing communication in a new culture requires some thought. What do you think about when you travel to a country you've never visited before or when you prepare to meet a business colleague or customer from another culture? Most of us will certainly think about the language and cultural differences if we travel to other countries. It's both exciting and sometimes daunting—especially if we are going to a place we consider to be very different from where we live and work. More than likely, we do our best to learn a few words in the country's language and try to learn some of their customs as well. That is definitely a key element to bridging the cultural gap; however, it goes beyond that. There are many layers and contexts to communication, which ultimately affects how others perceive us. We communicate in ways we probably aren't even aware of. Our very presence is a form of communication; the way we look, our choice of attire, and how we present ourselves says something to other people about us.

This is why, when doing business in another country or with people from another country, we need to anticipate how others are likely to perceive *everything* about us—including any "strikes" there may be against us (as originally discussed in Chapter 3). It comprises our language, our communication style differences, and the various tonality and body language preferences we have. It even includes any preconceived conceptions about the topic we're discussing. Has anything happened in the past, as a result of interpersonal, phone, or e-mail interactions, that may have created a level of animosity? If so, what is the best way to position your approach and communication to create a new perception? One good way to think about this is to step into the other person's shoes, both as a culture and as a businessperson. What would you expect or want to hear if you were that person? What would you like to have happen?

Thinking like another person is the key in any type of business interaction—within *or* outside of your own culture—whether you are in management, sales, or another profession. However, it becomes increasingly important to do this when you find yourself in a cross-cultural situation. For example, when I present to different cultures, I think about the appropriate communication styles to use for that culture. I consider what could potentially be offensive in that culture and choose my words, tone of voice, and body language or gestures carefully. Although we're not always even aware of them, gestures can be your worst enemy. In fact, one gesture can mean something very different from one culture to the next. And it's the fastest way to offend someone, albeit unintentionally. Unfortunately, cultural homogenization doesn't seem to afford much lenience for unintentionally offending someone with gestures. Gesture offense is one big taboo that can be very difficult to recover from. This is definitely an area to remain aware of, and avoiding offensive gestures certainly goes a long way in minimizing ineffective communication. A basic guideline is to use only open-handed gestures. Don't point with your index finger, don't use the thumbs up or thumbs down sign, and don't use the OK sign. Although this sign actually means "okay" in the United States, it means "zero" in France, means "money" in Japan, and is a very obscene gesture in Brazil!

Most important, I think about how *my audience*—whether it is one person or 1,000—*may react* to what I'm going to say and how I plan to say it. As a result, I might choose to say something very differently than I originally planned, or I might decide to omit something altogether.

For example, I make it a point to avoid religious, political, and sensitive economic issues when I know they may be controversial.

Anticipating other people's reactions can be very helpful, because their reactions are how you can gauge whether you've been successful or not. Keep in mind that you can determine the communication's meaning by the response you get. So observing that response will guide you every step of the way—*if you pay attention.* In this way, cross-cultural interactions often become a dance of shifting and adjusting. They involve a flow of learning and understanding that ultimately leads to successful relationships. This tendency applies to all kinds of interactions—in person, on the phone, and via e-mail.

I often tell the people I coach in presentation skills, "It's not about how you are doing; it's about how *they* are doing." In other words, are they with you or not? Do they understand what you're saying, or do they look confused? What is their body language telling you? How do they respond with their eyes? Keep the following maxim in mind: "Real eyes" can help you realize. If they aren't receiving your message the way you anticipated, that is your clue to change your approach.

Truly excellent communicators think about how to maximize their communication *in advance* of presenting. Of course, even with the best intentions, we can't prepare for everything. That is when we use the 80 percent rule. Do 80 percent of the preparation, and the remaining 20 percent will take care of itself. There will always be some unexpected reactions or surprises; that's what makes communication interesting. The point is, if someone is with you, you can easily manage the unexpected without going in reactive circles. If you build a strong foundation of understanding, the rest will basically be explanation and clarification. Receiving verification that you've been understood in the *way you intended* is extremely important in cross-cultural interactions.

Countries' and cultures' business and social expectations can differ vastly. This is why you want to learn as much as you can about the ones you visit or work with. The most basic thing to know is your geography and where the countries you visit or work with are located. One of the biggest complaints we hear multiculturally is that that people from other countries don't even know where they are located on a map. So inform yourself about other countries' power and control systems (laws, enforcement, rules, business hierarchy), their value systems (what's important to them), the appropriate attire for various occasions, the preferred business and social protocol, and the general attitude about discussing family, politics, and the economy, to name a few. These are just a few of the topics where it's all too easy to get off on the wrong foot and become reactive.

Learn about how formality, hierarchy, and timing can affect business and social interactions, especially during negotiations and decision making. Find out if a culture is more formal and expressive or more direct and to the point. It's crucial that the people with whom you're communicating do not perceive you as too aggressive or impatient in your business approach. Business often takes longer with people from other cultures and countries. Be aware that in many team-focused or we-oriented cultures, it's essential not to come across as too egocentric or I-oriented. All of these things can affect your business style and marketing approach.

Remember as well that as cultures are homogenizing, tendencies and expectations are constantly changing. Don't be surprised if things are different than you anticipated.

If you learn about the cultures you interact with, proactively prepare, and maximize your effective communication, you've taken a big step toward developing successful cross-cultural relationships. It's not all that difficult, and it's so much more fun, productive, and enjoyable for everyone than being reactive.

KEY TWO

Rapport Secrets to Bridge the Cultural Gap

In Person, on the Phone, and by E-Mail

The chapters in Key Two will cover what you must be aware of in order to establish multicultural rapport. We all communicate by using words, our tone of voice, and body language; however, our native or mother tongue language strongly influences just how we use these three things in our communication. Some cultures place a strong emphasis on *what* is said by the words we use, whereas others pay closer attention to *how* we say something with our tone of voice and body language.

Creating rapport is essential when meeting someone new. Establishing this helps you begin to build a common bond that leads to respect, trust, and understanding. It is one of the most important elements in cross-cultural relationships—because everyone knows how uncomfortable it is to be out of rapport.

Awareness is the first step! Part of this process involves learning to adjust your communication style to create a comfort zone with people from different cultures. This may include choosing your words, tone of voice, or body language carefully and changing them as the situation or interaction dictates. If you can find things you have in common with the other person or people—and be open to understanding any differences—you'll be well on your way to building rapport.

If you have good rapport with someone and something goes wrong, that person will be more likely to blame the circumstance or situation. If you have poor rapport with someone, he or she will be more likely to blame you. It's as simple as that.

CHAPTER

7

It's a Matter of Respect

Create Cultural Trust and Understanding

Establishing respect between individuals from different cultures isn't always as easy as we may think it will be. There are many degrees of respect—from the most basic to which every human being is entitled, to a deeper respect that can take years to develop. And when you combine these varying levels with the different multicultural expectations surrounding respect, the process can be even more challenging.

At times, it's difficult to determine whether we are respected or not. We usually share a degree of general respect for the individuals with whom we are interacting for a common purpose in social and business interactions. However, deeper levels of respect take on many forms and come in many shades—and it's possible to respect certain personal attributes and not others. For instance, we can respect someone because of a specialized ability and at the same time not respect the way that person handles certain things. We can respect someone because of his or her title, degree, age, position, or hierarchy and completely disrespect his or her behavior in some way. We can respect or even admire a person's business savvy and yet wonder why that person's personal life is in chaos.

We can develop *genuine* respect only over a period time. That time varies with each individual and with every culture. In various cultures, some levels of respect are more superficial than others. For instance,

I learned when I first lived in Zurich, Switzerland, that true friendship is slower to develop than it is in the United States. Much of that is because friendship in the Swiss German culture is based on deeper levels of respect for and knowledge about another person. Consequently, friendships grow stronger as respect develops, and they don't necessarily start off with the kind of immediate closeness that some American relationships tend to. The respect that the Swiss develop for one another usually needs to be well rounded in a variety of ways. They like to know that you are genuine, that you will keep your word, and that you can be trusted, all of which comes with the experience of knowing each other over time.

Indeed, many Europeans scoff when U.S. Americans claim to make good friends so quickly. When you think about it, it's fairly common to hear an American casually say something like, "A good friend of mine, whom I met skiing a few weeks ago, is coming to visit next month." The European response might be, "How could someone you just met a few weeks ago possibly be a 'good friend'? You have known that person for only a few weeks!" Developing good friendships so quickly may sound superficial to those in Europe, Asia, Latin America, the Middle East, and many other parts of the world. It is even more superficial to them when U.S. Americans refer to someone they recently met as a close friend. To most Europeans, a close friend is someone who is akin to family. The same typically applies in the workplace. In the United States, people are more likely to quickly become friends with coworkers, whereas people in many other countries may prefer to keep these relationships more professional.

A Swiss friend once told me that when I truly made a close friend of someone of Swiss origin, then that person would be a friend for life—and I would be like family to him or her. I have many friends in Switzerland, even some good friends; however, there is only one whom I consider a really *close* friend—and that friendship extends to her entire family. I *am* family to them, and they *are* family to me and my entire family. I refer to my close friend as my sister, and she does the same. But in true Swiss fashion, that relationship came about as a result of several years of trust, understanding, and earned respect for each other. She was hired to be my French-English business translator when I worked in Geneva, so of course we worked very closely together and our friendship grew. Our daughters also became friends, and now some 20 years later, we are all truly family to one another.

For the most part, friendships in countries outside the United States take time to build and are strongly based on respect. As a result, everything relating to communication, sales, and negotiations will likely take more time. This is especially true in many of the Asian cultures. When we work with companies that sell and negotiate in various Asian countries, we tell them that getting to know, understand, and ultimately trust one another is the precursor to making any sort of sale. They might need to take two or even three visits to the country to develop the relationship and move forward with the business at hand. The U.S. business culture is typically faster paced, with a push to get deals done immediately. As a result, it is important to adjust your expectations regarding how long something will take to avoid becoming frustrated and impatient.

It's crucial when developing working relationships with other cultures that we be able to respect ways of doing things that may be quite different from our own. They may even be so different that they're uncomfortable at times. We don't necessarily have to *like* the way that cultures other than our own do things; however, we do have to *respect* that their methods and approaches are as valid as our own. When it comes to distinct business styles, there is not right or wrong; there's just different. Once we attain that level of acceptance, we can further establish respect—for the values and distinctions of unique individuals in unique cultures, and for the cultural values, business hierarchy, customary titles, social rituals, cultural timing, appropriate behavior, protocol, and even food and drink preferences. Showing that we acknowledge and are comfortable with these differences—as well as willing to participate in what is important to another culture—goes a long way in creating mutual trust, understanding, and respect.

The very nature of human respect is centered on our ability to trust one another. If we don't have this, it becomes very difficult to accomplish anything. Trust is at the core of all relationships—trust in what is said, in what is done, and in the integrity of another person, company, or country. No matter what culture you work and live in, *trust* is a word that is close to everyone's heart. It is also something that needs to be earned—and that process is more difficult with some individuals, and in some cultures, than others.

The first step of earning trust is ensuring that the parties involved are able to *understand* one another. Understanding in this sense doesn't necessarily mean agreeing; it just means that the people or companies involved in the interaction understand the meaning behind what both have communicated. Many members of various Asian cultures will even nod their heads and say, "Yes," as a sign that they have understood what has been said. This absolutely *does not* mean that they *agree with* what has been said. On the contrary, they may totally disagree; it simply indicates that they've understood or *heard* what the other person has communicated. As you might imagine, this can throw off even the most astute negotiator. One of our U.S.-based customers once thought they had come to an agreement in a negotiation and flew to China with the final contract. Come to find out, the Chinese delegation had simply agreed that they had liked what was presented the first time and were ready for a follow-up presentation!

On a very basic level, understanding one another simply means that there has been no misunderstanding. There is clarity about what both parties have communicated and understood. That could possibly lead to agreement, but even if it doesn't—it's certainly a step in the right direction. This basic level of harmony will eventually lead to an understanding *between* the individuals or parties involved, which can help develop to a deeper level—that, with time, will ultimately lead to trust. Having a basis of understanding and trust allows a genuine sense of respect to develop. This respect will strengthen over time as the relationship matures, as long as the trust, understanding, and integrity remain intact.

CHAPTER

8

Develop Rapport

The Most Important Element in Cross-Cultural Relationships

What is rapport? This term is difficult for most people to define, because it's more of a *feeling* than anything else. You know when you feel it, and you know when you don't. You can even feel it with a perfect stranger when you least expect it.

How many times while standing in line at the grocery store or movie theater or waiting at the airport have you struck up a conversation with a complete stranger? You may begin talking about something that is of interest to both of you, or nothing special at all—just making conversation. At that moment in time, you feel that you have something in common with that person. You have *connected* with that person, and you feel comfortable with him or her. There is a natural feeling of similarity and trust for that brief interval together.

And even if you never see that person again, you had complete rapport with a perfect stranger as your paths crossed. When you part ways, you probably think to yourself, "That was a nice guy [or woman]." And the other person is probably thinking the same thing about you. You have just experienced rapport in its purest form. It's a connection—a natural feeling of comfort, similarity, and trust with someone you had never met before—for that instant in time. And everyone has had that *feeling* of rapport at one time or another.

The question is: Why do we have rapport with some people and not with others? Why is it so easy with certain individuals and so difficult with others? And why, sometimes when we really *want* to have rapport with someone, isn't it there?

We need to keep in mind that rapport is a *feeling*, a nebulous sensation that can't be specifically defined. It's difficult to know why it sometimes happens so naturally and why it sometimes doesn't happen at all. Rapport is created because of characteristics, opinions, attitudes, experiences, and countless other things that individuals have in common. This commonality can take on a broader meaning based on an individual's core layers of similarity, or it can simply come as a result of a more immediate sense of camaraderie, like a weather-related delay at the airport. It can develop because of similar life experiences related to our native culture or because of likeness in appearance. It can be because we have common interests with someone else. It can be because we're both in the same situation at the same time, or it could be due to numerous other things, too many to mention.

I remember being relinquished to the stairwell on the 42nd floor of a skyscraper once as an imminent tornado was heading for Dallas. For three hours, everyone who was on the floor together had one goal in common: working our way down the stairs to the parking garage! Because of the situation, there was an unspoken rapport between everyone. We made our way down systematically, with humor and camaraderie, with everyone helping each other to make it out okay.

Many individual factors contribute to that feeling of rapport. Yet ultimately, it's based on a connection or understanding between two or more individuals. It's the common bond that develops at a *deep, unconscious level*. It is undoubtedly one of the most important elements in relationships, especially cross-cultural relationships. Everyone knows how uncomfortable it is to be out of rapport with someone, regardless of his or her culture. There are many differences to overcome in multicultural relationships; however, if people *like* one another, their similarities emerge and the differences become less important.

If you are a businessperson involved in sales, marketing, or virtually any other industry in the corporate spectrum, the following *three simple steps* are essential to your success.

1. **Develop rapport.**

   You need to have rapport with someone to further the relationship and help him or her. If you don't develop this basic connection from the very beginning, the other person isn't likely to feel comfortable with you. And if he or she doesn't feel comfortable with you, it's difficult to accomplish anything together.

2. **Find out the other person's needs.**

   Establishing rapport with someone makes it easier for you to discover what that person needs and then help him or her achieve it. You can't help someone if you don't know what's needed—and because sometimes *the other person* doesn't even know what's needed, it's often up to you to figure it out together.

3. **Fulfill the other person's needs.**

   Once you know what someone needs, you can help fulfill that need; that is, help the person achieve, accomplish, or get what's wanted. This is the goal, the outcome, the purpose of your involvement. We are all basically in the business of *fulfillment* of one kind or another.

These three steps are the foundation for all business relationships. They look different from one industry to the next, and they may sometimes happen unconsciously and effortlessly. However, they require a conscious endeavor more often than not, especially when cross-cultural relationships come into play.

A couple of important points to keep in mind about rapport:

- If you have good rapport with someone and something goes wrong, that person is more likely to blame the situation or circumstance. Why? Because that person likes *you*. So this is a good thing—something that's definitely working in your favor.

- If you have poor rapport with someone and something goes wrong, that person is more likely to blame you than the situation—for the opposite reason, of course: because he or she doesn't like you.

Building rapport is challenging; determining how to do it is unique to each individual in every culture. The key is to know what is likely to be important to another person or culture and then find things in common to talk about. People tend to like people who are like themselves, with similar interests and expectations. Be a good listener and look for shared points in common. Remember *we have two ears and one mouth for a reason*, and rapport is created as much by listening as by talking! The expectations people have in terms of having their needs fulfilled also varies from culture to culture. Some cultures tend to be more *process-oriented*; that is, the process and steps along the way to fulfillment are equally as important as the outcome. Process, protocol, and the way things are done are very important to many of the Asian cultures. Other cultures, including U.S. culture, tend to be more *outcome-oriented*. As long as they achieve the requisite outcome, the process of how you get there isn't all that important.

What is most important is that you develop *some* level of rapport. It may not always come naturally; however, by getting to know someone, discovering similarities, finding things in common, showing an interest, being sincere, and working toward fulfilling that person's needs, you have taken the first steps in being successful in your multicultural rapport. The next step is to learn to adapt your style and approach as necessary for a *specific* culture, which we will discuss in the following chapter.

9

Adapt Your Style

Awareness Is the First Step!

How do you develop cultural rapport? Sometimes you need to adapt your style. People who are like each other tend to like each other. We are comfortable with what we are familiar with.

On April 25, 2005, the *Dallas Morning News* printed a picture of President George W. Bush and the Saudi Crown Prince Abdullah strolling, *hand in hand*, through the bluebonnets on his ranch in Crawford, Texas. It brought to mind two questions. First, was it really President Bush's idea to walk with Crown Prince Abdullah while holding hands? Second, how many of my readers think that President Bush was really *comfortable* doing it? The answer to both questions is most likely, "No." So, what was the reason for the cozy stroll, especially with the obvious presence of the press? After all, they weren't in Saudi Arabia—and two men strolling hand in hand isn't a common thing to do—or see—in Texas!

It was apparent that President Bush was aware of the expected cultural protocol for the Crown Prince's visit. Since Abdullah was visiting President Bush at his home, this was sign of a *personal friendship* in addition to that of two leaders meeting for political purposes. President Bush and the Crown Prince had a friendship that dictated certain gestures of closeness and camaraderie. Had President Bush not taken Crown Prince Abdullah's hand, it may have conveyed to the Crown Prince that their friendship wasn't as close as he had thought. Holding hands while walking is customary and natural between male friends in Saudi Arabia.

We all need to adapt our style sometimes, but the question often becomes: *Who* should adapt and *where?* Most have heard the common adage, "When in Rome, do as the Romans!" Therefore, it might seem that since the Crown Prince was visiting President Bush's home in the United States, *he* would have adapted to the protocol of the United States and Texas. If the situation had been reversed—and President Bush was visiting the Crown Prince at his palace in Saudi Arabia—it would make sense that President Bush would adapt to the Saudi culture's protocol. However, the importance of the Crown Prince's visit and the nature of the friendship between the two men compelled President

Figure 9.1
**President George W. Bush and Saudi Crown Prince Abdullah
strolling hand in hand through the bluebonnets**
Photo by the *Dallas Morning News*

Bush to take the necessary steps to create a warm, comfortable rapport by honoring their friendship in the customary Saudi manner. In doing so, he extended his respect to the Crown Prince.

"When in Rome" is a safe place to start when creating rapport; however, there are no hard-and-fast rules. Frequently, both parties will initially adapt and ultimately find a comfortable rapport where they can meet somewhere in the middle of the cultural customs. And they often do so even without knowing what is customary for a specific culture.

Awareness is always the first and most important step. You can find a lot of rapport clues simply by observing interpersonal relationships. Is another culture more or less formal than your own? Is the body language of that culture's people demonstrative or less so? Is their behavior assertive or a little more apprehensive? Do they tend to speak loudly or softly? Is there much rapport building small talk, or are they more direct and to the point? Is their posture tall and upright or more relaxed? Posture is a good indicator of someone's overall communication style and approach. Is the standard greeting a handshake, a bow, a kiss on the cheek, or possibly a hug? Obviously, the diversity laws vary from country to country. I found this out very quickly in Geneva, Switzerland, where there are three kisses on the cheek for both greetings and departures. There are a lot of things you can learn just by observing.

Once you are aware of how people relate to one another in person, it's a simple matter of "matching and mirroring": to copy, match, or mirror the observed behavior and style. Follow the formality, greetings, and conversation style the other people are using. Adjust your tone of voice to be louder and more assertive or softer and a little more passive. Assume a similar posture and body language. If the other person uses expressive gestures, be more expressive with yours. If the other party uses very few gestures, limit yours. If greeted with a gentler handshake, be gentler with yours. Many of us have been taught that a firm handshake is the *only* kind of handshake. People in Texas even say that there are three types of handshakes: gentle, firm, and Texan, which is double firm! However, some cultures—including many Asian ones—consider overly firm handshakes to be aggressive. And because your goal is to develop a comfortable relationship, you may be required to do some adapting.

Face-to-face relationships are the easiest by far to observe and with which to establish rapport. Sometimes, though, the behavior you observe requires a little explanation. A few years ago, we helped a company relocate 250 Japanese engineers to their U.S. headquarters in Dallas. One of the things that really puzzled the Japanese was how coworkers greeted one another in the workplace. They would pass in the hall and say, "Hi, how are you?" and then continue walking without waiting for an answer. The Japanese engineers would turn around to answer the question, and their coworkers were halfway down the hall. To the Japanese, it seemed rude to ask people how they were doing and not wait for an answer. We had to explain that in the United States, "How are you?" really isn't a question that you wait for an answer to. It's simply *part* of the greeting "Hi." And the other person gives the typical reply of "Fine" as you both continue on your way without missing a beat!

Although it's not quite as effective as seeing or talking with someone face to face, talking and listening on the phone can help you figure out how to establish rapport, especially phone rapport. Is the caller direct and to the point, or is there some small talk first? Does the person talk fast or more slowly and deliberately? Does the speaker vary his or her tone of voice or use very little tonality? How does the person answer the phone, and what is the typical greeting?

When I first started working in Switzerland, I was surprised that people working in the Swiss German part of the country simply stated their last name when they answered the phone. For example, I would answer the phone by saying, "Cotton," and nothing more. They also didn't ask, "How are you?" as part of the initial phone greeting. I'll never forget the time I returned a call to a gentleman from a pharmaceutical company in Basel, Switzerland. I said, "Hello, Mr. _____. How are you today?" He promptly replied, "None of your damn business! Now the reason I called . . ." He then proceeded with what he had to say, as though nothing had happened, and I did the same. We ended up working with their company, and surprisingly, he really was a very nice guy! Lesson learned. I found out that much of northern Europe felt the same way about the question, "How are you?" That inquiry seems superficial to them, because the answer is usually, "I'm fine," whether you are or not! No one gives a true answer, and who really cares anyway? Consequently, I've never asked it again in the northern European cultures, unless someone else asked me first.

Establishing phone rapport is a matter of pacing and leading with the initial phone communication style. You want to start the conversation at a pace that's similar to the other person's, and then gradually lead the conversation to a pace that is comfortable for both of you.

If the other person speaks more expressively, use a more expressive tone yourself. If he or she speaks with less animation, then don't be overly animated when you speak. If the other person likes a little small talk, be more social at the beginning of the call. But if the other person is direct and to the point, don't waste his or her time with small talk.

We recently conducted cross-cultural training for a company that had business locations in Dallas and New York City. The goal of this training was to enable better cross-cultural communication for both cities' business cultures. Most of the communication was virtual, done via phone, e-mail, and text. The phone communication created the biggest challenge. The Dallas office had a female employee we'll call Nellie Brown. Nellie was a "native Texan" with a charming Southern accent—and one of the sweetest ladies you would ever want to meet. She would call the New York office and sincerely say, "Hi, y'all! This is Nellie Brown in Daaallas. How's y'all's weather up there? I hear y'all have had an awful lot of snow! It must be pretty cold. How do y'all manage with all that?" Her extended social conversation drove the New York office crazy! They liked Nellie, but her phone calls were lengthy and, in their words, had too much "fluff." They thought that Nellie, and others down in the Dallas office, wasted their time on the phone.

However, the opposite was true when people from the New York office would call the Dallas office. They were so direct about what they wanted that the Dallas office called them impolite and thought they sounded rude and antisocial. It seemed to the Dallas office that the New Yorkers were focused solely on the purpose of the call and didn't care about the relationship between colleagues or coworkers. It was a true clash, between very different cultures—both of which were in the United States.

After the training, both the New York and the Dallas office began to adapt their phone rapport style. They made efforts to pace and lead with each other's conversations, keeping in mind both the call's purpose and the relationship between coworkers.

One day, a New York coworker called and surprised Nellie when she asked how her daughter's wedding had gone. The coworker had engaged in a *personal discussion* even before the business at hand had been addressed. Nellie was astonished that she had asked about a topic about which Nellie assumed her coworker had absolutely no interest. I told Nellie that her coworker really *was* interested in some of the personal things that she talked about; their calls had just been too time-consuming in the past. Now that Nellie was more direct and to the point, her coworker had a little more time to socially chat a bit. The communication between the two offices had found a comfortable phone rapport that worked for both the New York and Dallas communication styles.

E-mail has rapidly become the most commonly used form of business communication. It's often easier than a phone call, especially with different time zones or when you're trying to avoid calling a person who tends to be long winded. There is also a "paper trail" of what has been said, and people tend to check their e-mail more often than their phone messages. In terms of multicultural communication, people typically understand second languages better when they read them than they do when they speak them. They can also use the e-mail dictionary, if necessary, without being intimidated.

We meet, greet, and establish rapport by e-mail ever more frequently in today's global business environment. Developing e-mail rapport is a relationship skill, just like any other form of communication. Observing how the sender writes an e-mail can give the receiver many clues as to how to create e-mail rapport, especially when it comes to new e-mail relationships. Are the exchanges formal or informal? Is there some social small talk or rapport building at the beginning of the e-mail about how you are doing, the weather, or something you have in common, or do they get directly to the point? Are they rather expressive or less so? Are the e-mails organized with bullets and numbers, or are they in paragraph form? Do they use fancy fonts, bold, and color or a simple black font? Is the writing very descriptive or fairly simple and straightforward? Does the e-mail end with *Sincerely, Regards, Best regards, Kind regards, Warmest regards*, or no regards at all? There are numerous ways to put personality into e-mail. When it comes to e-mail rapport, it's best to model the sender. Eventually, rapport will find the middle road that is comfortable for all parties involved.

Texting is another kind of communication that has quickly gained popularity—not only in the social realm, but in business exchanges as well. Texting is a less expensive way to stay connected when travelling internationally than making a phone call. And thanks to younger generations' influence, texting is gaining a legitimate place in global business. Many young people believe it's disrespectful to leave a voice mail when a text will do! As with all other kinds of interaction, observing someone's text communication style will give you the rapport clues you need for it. Business text protocol is in its infancy, so it's constantly becoming more defined. There is now an entire text dictionary similar to the old shorthand. The initial point of texting was to not have to worry about typing full words or using proper spelling and grammar. However, that doesn't hold true for everyone. Some businesspeople are using texts as a replacement for e-mails or phone calls. They choose to write their texts more professionally, whereas others abbreviate and use text jargon such as "10Q" for "thank you," "@TEOTD" for "at the end of the day," or "BFN" for "bye for now," and they don't worry about spelling or grammar. This will be discussed in more detail in Chapter 23.

So how do we know what is appropriate for text rapport? Once again, you model the sender! In both e-mail and text communications, the sender is telling you his or her *preferred* style for e-mails and texts. That is your cue to send a similar style of text or e-mail in return. Someone who texts with abbreviations and doesn't worry about grammar or spelling is indicating a preference for directness and not wanting to waste time on lengthy texts. Of course, you could make the argument that this is less professional and not business-like, so it is certainly a judgment call. On the other end of the spectrum, someone who sends a more formal and descriptive text is signaling a preference for a less direct, more conversational style and possibly a preference for more detail. This person is also sending the message that he or she likes a more conventional and professional written style.

A caveat with regard to e-mail and text communication: Neither is the best method to use when emotions are running high. It's all too easy to let emotions spill into the e-mail or text. If you offend someone in person, there is no documentation of what the other person "really said." The same applies to communication on the phone, unless you leave a voice message. However, if you offend someone in an e-mail or text, the recipient can read it over and over again—and it usually makes the person feel worse with each subsequent reading!

No matter what culture you are from, with simple observation and listening, you can adapt to make your multicultural interactions successful in person, on the phone, and in your written communication.

And always remember: Awareness is the *first*, the *most important*, and the *easiest* step!

Words, Tonality, and Body Language

The Three Methods of Communication That Vary with Every Culture

By and large, human beings use three different methods to communicate our thoughts: our words, our tone of voice, and our body language. The way in which we use these methods determines how well others will receive our message. Its meaning is based on the response we get, which tells us how well we used the three methods to convey our message.

The first method we use to communicate is our words.

What to Keep in Mind about Words

- Words are an "assigned sound" that represent something in various languages.

- Words are symbols assigned to an *association of ideas* that means something.

- Words are entirely *subjective*.

- Words very rarely mean exactly what you think they do to another person.

- The meaning of a word varies with every person, language, and culture.

And when you compound all of these details pertaining to words with the translations from language to language, they become even *more* subjective. Ask 10 different people what the word *culture* means, and you will likely get 10 different answers ranging from "ethnic" to "etiquette"! The concept of culture can refer to the social culture, the corporate culture, or even to being cultured in terms of one's education and refined appreciation of the arts. Miscommunication as a result of the words used is a constant challenge during an exchange—whether it's in person, via phone, or via e-mail, text, or some other form of written communication.

Words don't always translate precisely when you're going from one language to another either. Words that are translated to a different language seldom have the same meaning they did in the original language. For example, English and French speakers both use the word *special*, and it is spelled exactly the same in both languages. If you say that "someone is *special* to you" in English, it means that that person is endeared to you in some way. However, when the word is used in French in that context, it is meant to indicate that someone is a little weird or strange. I made the mistake of giving a French girlfriend a birthday card that said she was a "special person" and ended up spending the next half hour explaining what I meant by it! Furthermore, the use of a translated word can often be out of context with what is being said—and context challenges can happen even when the same language is spoken. In American English, the phrase *to table it* usually means to put something away and come back to it later. In British English, it means to put it on the table and deal with it now—exactly the opposite meaning!

People in the Southern U.S. commonly use a term rarely heard in the North: "I might could have." The first time I heard it, I had no idea what they were talking about. I later found out it meant, "I might *have been* able to." That's confusion with American English in different parts of the same country. Another word that is commonly used by females in the South is the word *Hon*. They will say something like, "Hon, would you like some help with that?" You might think it was a term of endearment coming from the word *honey*, but they often use it with complete strangers!

The second method we use to communicate is our tone of voice, or tonality.

Four Major Things Affect Tonality

1. **Tempo:** How fast or slow we speak

   Some cultures, such as the Latin-based or romantic language cultures, tend to speak more rapidly than other cultures. However, tempo is also a very individual quality in the communication style of most languages.

2. **Tone:** The range of high and low in our tone of voice as we communicate

   Some cultures use more of the tonal range than do others. Italian and many of the other romantic language cultures tend to use a varied tonality with more highs and lows. On the other hand, the Germans and Scandinavians tend to use a less varied tonality with fewer highs and lows.

3. **Volume:** how loudly or softly we speak

   Some cultures, such as romantic language cultures, naturally speak at a higher volume than others, whereas many Asian cultures tend to speak more softly in their normal communication.

4. **Timbre:** the intonation, resonance, and inflection used in our speech

   Many of the romantic language cultures are inclined to use a more expressive intonation and inflection in their communication compared with some other cultures.

Our tone of voice *modifies* our words and gives them credibility. It gives greater meaning and emphasis to what we've said. Tonality can even completely change the meaning of our words. For example, if someone screams, "I love you!" in a harsh, angry-sounding voice, it probably doesn't convey what the words intended. The message wasn't credible, because the words and tonality weren't congruent. However, if someone uttered the same phrase in a gentle, soothing voice, the message's meaning dramatically changes.

Tonality is a very powerful tool in communication. In various Asian cultures' languages and dialects, tone of voice and word inflection can convey numerous different meanings for a single word. We once had a

Korean in one of our classes say the word for "tree," *namu*, with a slightly different inflection 10 or so times—and it meant something different each time. The amazing thing was that after the first two or three words, it was nearly impossible for the rest of us to even hear the difference! These cultures listen very carefully for the slight distinctions and alterations in tonality and inflection that may indicate different meanings and nuances to the words used.

Tonality is very important to many cultures, not just the aforementioned Asian ones.

In fact, inflection and tonality can alter the way people perceive communication in *most* languages. Consider how emphasizing a different word in just one phrase can give it an entirely difference nuance or meaning:

"*I* really need you to help me."

"I *really* need you to help me."

"I really *need* you to help me."

"I really need *you* to help me."

"I really need you *to* help me."

"I really need you to *help* me."

"I really need you to help *me*."

The tones that certain cultures use—especially those that lean toward significantly softer or louder tonalities—may affect how other cultures perceive them. Because many of the Asian cultures tend to talk in lower tones, people might see them as having a more passive communication style. On the other side of the spectrum are countries and areas such as the United States, southern Europe, and Latin America—people from these cultures tend to talk louder and therefore might be perceived as being more assertive, or even aggressive, communicators. Asian individuals might even view people from these louder, more assertive cultures as egotistical or overly confident, whereas those from U.S., southern European, and Latin American cultures might perceive people from the softer, more passive cultures as unsure of themselves or less confident. People from all these cultures might be choosing to use *exactly the same* words, but the tonality, inflection, and emphasis give a different implication and connotation to what has been said.

Accents also fall into the category of tonality, especially since almost everyone has a preference for a particular accent in a given language. For instance, one of our customers, a well-known European bank, wanted to hire an English-speaking marketing director for their English-speaking customers. A woman from Louisiana who was living in Europe applied for the job. She was by far the most qualified candidate; however, the company wouldn't hire her because, to them, her Louisiana accent made her sound "ignorant." Instead, they gave the job to someone who spoke English with a German accent.

The third method we use to communicate is our physiology or body language.

Body Language Includes Many Things

- Facial expressions
- Gestures
- Posture
- Mannerisms
- Eye contact
- Social etiquette protocol
- Business etiquette protocol

Body language modifies both our words' meaning and our tonality. It generates credibility and is the number one factor for determining our congruency. And if we aren't congruent, we aren't believable; it's as simple as that. Even if our words and tonality are communicating in unison, we won't seem sincere if our body language is conveying something different. For example, if a professional speaker has poor posture, doesn't make any eye contact with the audience, and uses no expressive gestures whatsoever, it is very difficult for people to view him as credible and congruent. He will likely be unable to engage the audience, no matter how brilliant his words and tonality.

Do these three methods we use to convey what we think and feel—words, tonality, and body language—all have an equal value in the communication process? How heavily does each factor weigh in conveying what we want to say to others? If we assume a total of 100 percent in face-to-face communication, how much value we should give to each element?

When we ask this question in our cross-cultural communication classes, the answers we get vary tremendously. Some break it down as 20 percent for words, 40 percent for tonality, and 40 percent for body language. Others may say it's 50 percent for words, 25 percent for tonality, and 25 percent for body language. Still others might believe it to be 5 percent for words, 20 percent for tonality, and 75 percent for body language. Then, there is always the balanced person who says it's 33 1/3 percent for words, 33 1/3 percent for tonality, and 33 1/3 percent for body language. The big question is, "Who's right?" And the answer is, "Everyone!" The value of words, tonality, and body language varies with every person, language, and culture. There is no right or wrong answer.

Many people who work in the field of communication will point to the fact that some books set the value at 7 percent for words, 38 percent for tonality, and 55 percent for body language (Figure 10.1). What they *don't* tell you is that those figures refer to global averages and don't reflect individual cultures' preferences. Most people are surprised by those percentages, even for a global average. They wonder, how can words be only 7 percent? In fact, the percentages are basically correct if you are referring to general face-to-face communication. Think about a time when someone told you he could do something, but his face was full of doubt and every fiber of his body language said, "No, I really can't!" Body language definitely speaks louder than words. It's just that the global averages don't account for all factors. For example, if the communication includes industry-specific or technical jargon, the percentage for words goes up and that for body language goes down.

It's also interesting to consider how tonality affects telephone communication. If you take away the body language, tonality becomes much more important; it literally *replaces* body language on the phone. People who work in customer service often say that if you smile on the phone, the person you are talking to will know it. The customer certainly can't

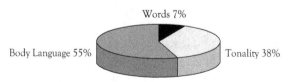

Figure 10.1
Global Communication Averages

see your smile; however, smiling does keep your face muscles relaxed. If your face is relaxed, your vocal cords are more relaxed. This makes your voice sound more pleasant, thereby letting the customer *hear* your smile. Communication experts say that tonality on the phone can have a value of up to 93 percent (calculating 38 percent tonality + 55 percent body language), with the words remaining at around 7 percent.

When you think about it, if the person you are talking to sounds totally disinterested, his or her tonality will probably convey more to you than the words being spoken. If I were to answer the phone and say, "Gayle Cotton, Circles Of Excellence, how can I help you?" in a tired, totally disinterested-sounding voice, the person on the other end certainly wouldn't think I was excited to have his or her business. On the phone, it really may not be *what* you said, but *how* you said it!

People around the world all use the same three methods to communicate. Our words, tone of voice, and body language are the common links that help us transfer our messages. How we use them determines how successful we will be in *transcending* culture.

CHAPTER
11

Understanding Communication

How Do You Describe a Tree?

Communication and the words we use are all about *association*—because words mean something different to every human being. They are entirely subjective and don't convey the exact same thing in any language or culture. It doesn't matter whether a word is from the same language or not; it's all about what someone *associates* with that word. The word *hot* will probably mean something quite different to someone who lives in Iceland than it does to someone who lives in Arizona. In Dallas, we always laugh when the weatherperson says we have a cold front coming through, which usually means the temperature will drop from 100 to 85 degrees farenheit (38 to 29 degrees celsius)!

Take, for example, the word *tree*. What does it mean? Since the word *tree* is a *symbol*, or an *assigned sound*, that represents what one associates with a tree, its meaning is determined by an individual's *interpretation* of that association.

We often ask attendees in our cross-cultural communication courses to describe what a tree is to them *without using* the word *tree*. They proceed to describe something with a big, brown trunk; long brown branches; and green leaves on the branches that turn brown and fall off in the autumn. What I just described is an association of ideas that represents a particular *type* of tree. Other attendees will describe a similar association of ideas for a tree and add various types of flowers, fruit, and nuts. We now have a variety of associations for different *types* of trees.

Soon, we start getting very diverse types of trees. Someone will describe a tree that has the attributes of a pine tree, and someone else will describe a palm or a weeping willow tree. People from various cultures will begin to describe trees from all over the world. We'll get descriptions for bonsai, date, persimmon, ginkgo, sassafras, locust, bombax, acacia, cabbage, stinkwood, travelers, sausage (a very interesting-looking tree!), dragon's blood, breadfruit, mulberry, olive, pagoda, tamboti, and even trees-from-heaven.

Eventually, we get descriptions for Christmas trees and even "family trees"! People get very good at describing the association of ideas that they know by the symbol or assigned sound that represents a tree—or the equivalent of tree in various languages:

Some Symbols for the Word *Tree*	
Albero, Italian	**Derakht**, Farsi
Árbol, Spanish	**Drzewo**, Polish
Arbre, French	**Ki**, Japanese
Baum, German	**Mti**, Swahili
Boom, Dutch	**Namu**, Korean
Cay, Vietnamese	**Tre**, Norwegian

The second question we ask our course attendees is, "What is the first tree that comes to mind when you think about the word *tree?*" People's answers have a great deal to do with what we associate with being a tree. The association that first comes to mind is often a tree from our childhood or a type of tree that's very familiar to us. However, it can also be a tree that is new, different, or recently caught our interest in some way. After our class exercise on trees, the first tree to come to mind is often one of the more unique trees that were new to many of the attendees.

The third question we pose is, "What would happen if two arborists were talking about fixing a sick tree, but one thought they were discussing a palm tree and the other thought they were discussing a pine tree?" The answer, of course, is that they would have a pretty tough time fixing that tree. They would need to clarify, describe, and ultimately agree upon what each of them was associating to the word *tree*.

This is often the situation we face in multicultural communication. The meaning one person associates with a particular word could be entirely different from the meaning another person has for that same word. This is compounded even further when someone is speaking in a second or third language or if the word has been translated.

Misunderstanding due to word association happens in business and social communication as well. Words don't always mean what we think they mean. There are numerous potential interpretations upon translations, as well as many exceptions to the rules of translation and definition. Anyone who works with translators knows this to be true.

I had an interesting experience with trees when I moved to Dallas. I had grown up in Washington State and had most recently lived in Switzerland, both places that have many types of pine trees. In fact, the Washington State car license plates read, "Welcome to Washington, the Evergreen State," so I was very familiar with evergreen trees. I knew that they were coniferous (that is, they have needles and cones) and that, per their name, they stayed green yearlong. I was also familiar with deciduous trees, which typically lose their leaves in the autumn. I was sure that I had both deciduous and coniferous trees in my yard at my home in Dallas.

In November, after my first hot summer in Dallas, my coniferous pine trees (or what I thought were pine trees) had lost all their needles. If you haven't seen a needleless pine tree, they are pretty funny looking—with all their little sticks and no branches. I thought that they may be dying, possibly because they didn't get enough water over the hot summer.

I decided to have an arborist come out to check them. He quickly looked at my trees and said, as a polite Texan would, "Ma'am, your trees are just fine." Looking rather puzzled, I replied, "They *can't be* fine. They are supposed to be evergreen trees, and they have no needles!" He responded with the fact that these were cypress trees, and cypress trees weren't evergreen in Texas. It was completely normal for them to lose their needles every autumn.

Most cypress trees are classified as coniferous in the northern United States; however, cypress trees in Texas are exceptions. They deviate from the definition of coniferous, because they aren't evergreen. What I had associated with coniferous trees was not the case in Texas. I was stuck with needleless pine trees throughout the winter. Fortunately, Texas winters aren't very long!

Since I was getting an education on trees in Texas, I decided to ask the arborist about my oak trees, which I had, of course, assumed were deciduous. They had all the characteristics of any deciduous tree I had ever seen; however, it was now well after the first frost, and their leaves were still green and lush. I was curious as to when they would lose their leaves.

To my surprise, the arborist told me that my trees were live oaks, and although they were *technically* deciduous, they didn't shed their leaves all at once like most deciduous trees. In Texas, they lose their old leaves after the new ones develop—so, in fact, they stay green all year long! I guess you could call *them* "evergreen."

As you might imagine, I was thoroughly confused by that point. Everything I thought I knew about trees had been turned completely upside down. I looked at the arborist and said, "Let me get this straight. My pine trees are going to lose their needles every year, but my oak trees will never shed their leaves?" He said, "That's correct, ma'am." I simply shook my head and replied, "Texas is one weird state!"

There can be so much confusion over what we associate to simple words. Everyone has such different ideas about their context and meaning. Exceptions to the rules (like coniferous and deciduous) make matters even more difficult. The context, and how a word is used, can create both miscommunication and misunderstanding.

This is precisely why, when communicating cross-culturally— whether we're doing so in the global business workplace or in social situations—it's important to remember that words are nothing more than symbols. They are an assigned sound to represent an association of ideas that can mean something different to everyone!

Figure 11.1
How Do *You* Describe a Tree?

The Impact of Mother Tongue Languages

It All Begins Here

Mother tongue languages are the basis for many of our cultural distinctions and behavioral styles. Language is one of the first things we hear when we are born, so it immediately begins to set a brain pattern for how we communicate. The rhythm, sound, and melody of our mother tongue language create the initial path for our shared cultural communication preferences.

Body language naturally moves with the *flow* of the language we are currently speaking. Our tone of voice sings the melody of this language—and we also think, and have ongoing internal conversations with ourselves, in this language.

True multilingual individuals can switch fairly effortlessly from thinking and speaking in one language to thinking and speaking in another. Typically the language you dream in is the one that is currently dominant—and this isn't necessarily your mother tongue language. I don't speak French fluently; however, after a few weeks in a French-speaking country, I begin to dream in French. That will usually continue for a few nights, upon my return to the United States.

The internal conversations we have with ourselves create communication style patterns that express themselves via our external communication. Linguistic research shows that the specific languages we speak affect both our tonality and body language. Our tone of voice moves high and low according to these languages' sound. Our body language accompanies the tonality to exemplify what is being said. The more variation in the highs and lows of our voice tone, the more expressive the body language tends to be.

People who speak several languages use a tonality and body language that reflect the melody or sound of the language they are currently speaking. When they switch to a different language, so do their tonality and body language—to then reflect *that* language's melody or sound. Words, tonality, and body language express, in unison, whatever language the person is speaking.

Almost everyone has experienced the unique communication styles of cultures that are different from their own. For example, a typical German will usually stand very tall, look you directly in the eye, have a firm one- or two-pump handshake, and be quite direct and to the point. Germans don't tend to be overly descriptive or use numerous adjectives and adverbs when they speak. They are easy to understand, because there are less communication nuances to figure out. They generally don't use overly demonstrative or expressive tonality and body language. Many additional cultures that speak Germanic languages, including the Austro-Bavarian, Scandinavian, Nordic, Icelandic, Yiddish, Anglo-Frisian, Flemish, and all variations of English, to name a few, have some of these similar characteristics.

Linguistic ethnography, anthropology, and social sciences generally conclude that language dynamics and social behavioral styles work together to mutually shape a culture's development. Studies have analyzed the impact that this has had on various cultures' communication styles and preferences. One particular analysis looked at how phrases from different languages appear on a tonal graph when spoken. These tonal graphs show how long it takes people to say a specific phrase in a language, the speech pattern of that language (hard and soft sounds, consonants and vowels), and how high or low the voice tone goes when saying the phrase. This has helped identify how a language influences a culture's communication patterns and behavior styles.

Figure 12.1 is an example of a German phrase on a tonal graph.

The vertical lines in the figure measure how long it takes to say the phrase, which is related to how many words are used to compose the phrase.

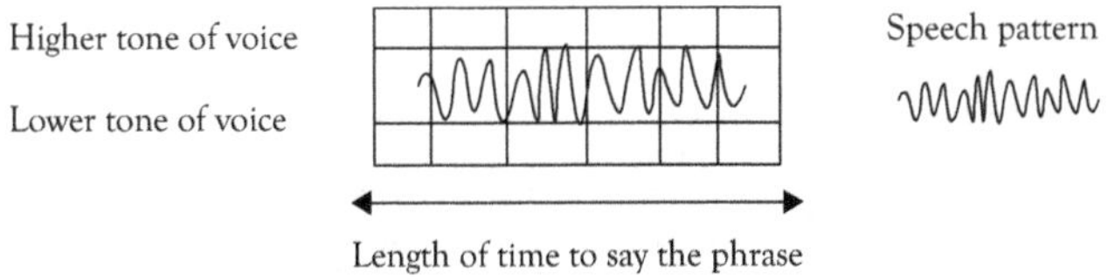

| Higher tone of voice | | Speech pattern |

Higher tone of voice

Lower tone of voice

Length of time to say the phrase

Figure 12.1
Example of a Tonal Graph for a German Phrase

It's apparent that this phrase didn't need the entire width of the graph to express what was said. This supports what I mentioned earlier—that most Germanic languages are quite precise, with words that typically mean precisely what they say. There are fewer nuances to what people are saying and fewer descriptive adjectives and adverbs.

The horizontal lines in the figure measure the levels of tonality, or how high and low the phrase's voice tones are. The upper horizontal line shows the higher levels of voice tone, and the lower horizontal line shows the lower levels of voice tone. The tonality is rather moderate in this case, as the voice tones don't cross the upper horizontal line (high tones) and just slightly cross the lower horizontal line (low tones).

The pointed, narrow curves of the tonal speech pattern signify a harder sound, or consonant, in the phrase. The wider, more rounded curves of the speech pattern signify a softer sound, or vowels, in the phrase. Since Germanic words often end in consonants or have silent vowels at the end, the speech pattern curves tend to be more narrow and pointed. The phrase has less melodic flow, which leads to less melodic flow in the tonality and body language. As a result, people from the Germanic language cultures generally use less tonality and body language in their communication style. However, body language varies on different occasions, as exemplified when Germans are at a beer garden giving their traditional toast of "Prost!"

The tendency of Germanic language cultures to be direct in spoken communication carries over into their written communication. These cultures see excessive tonality and body language as distracting, or even annoying. They feel the same way about overly descriptive and animated written communication. However, words and appropriate details—whether spoken or written—are very important. Words should be used wisely, be precise, and not be vague. All forms of communication should be well organized, to the point, and easy to follow.

Higher tone of voice

Lower tone of voice

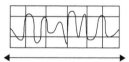

Speech pattern

Length of time to say the phrase

Figure 12.2

Example of a Tonal Graph for an Italian Phrase

At the opposite end of the spectrum from the Germanic tonal graph is the Latin-based or romantic language tonal graph. Figure 12.2 shows the same phrase in Italian that was exemplified on the Germanic tonal graph.

Again, the vertical lines measure in the figure how long it takes to say the phrase, which is related to how many words are used to compose it. This same phrase, spoken in Italian, uses the *entire width* of the graph to express what was said. Most Latin-based languages—including Spanish, Portuguese, French, Italian, Romanian, Catalan, Occitan, East Iberian, Indo-European, and West African French, among others—tend to use more words to say what they mean. Their words typically have more nuances, so they don't necessarily mean what you initially think they might. For example, the word *commerce* in French typically means the purchase and sale of goods or services; however, it can also mean to have an intellectual or social exchange between people. Romantic language cultures also enjoy making use of colorful, descriptive adjectives and adverbs when they speak.

The horizontal lines in the figure again measure the levels of tonality, or how high and low the voice tones are for the phrase. In this case, the tonality reaches the upper and lower horizontal lines, which shows that the person speaking uses a good deal of high and low voice tone.

The rounded, wide curves of the tonal speech pattern signify a softer sound, or lots of vowels in the phrase. Because words in the Italian language often end in vowels, these speech pattern curves tend to be very rounded and flow accordingly with the language's melody. Again, tonality and body language flow in unison with the language. The Italian language has considerable melody and, consequently, more tonality and body language.

An Italian once asked me, "What do you say to an Italian who is drowning?" I had no idea, until he smiled and said, "Keep talking!"

I thought for a moment and realized it made perfect sense. Their arm movements would effectively tread water while talking! Most of us have heard the saying, "If you tie an Italian's hands behind his back, he won't say a word!" It's very difficult for Italians, and other romantic language cultures, to communicate without using some kind of tonality and body language. It's no wonder that they like speakerphones; this method of communication gives them more freedom of movement to express themselves.

In general, people from the Latin-based language cultures use more tonality and body language in their communication style than do people from many other cultures. They also tend to be *less* direct and to the point in their spoken communication, which also carries over into their written communication. Without descriptive tonality and body language, communication often doesn't convey the intended message, and the same can happen with nonexpressive written communication. Tonality and body language are *part* of what words mean in these cultures. Of course, considering how many languages are Latin-based, there is a wide variation in the degree to which tonality and body language are used.

If you have ever wondered why the romantic language cultures love to dance, just look at their tonal graphs. The melodies and the flow of the various languages have led to the creation of many national dances, such as the tango, salsa, merengue, rhumba, cha-cha, and mambo. These dances are typically full of passion and emotion.

In contrast, the dance styles of many of the Germanic language cultures have less emotion and more deliberate movement. They are known for their folk dances, which are typically structured for group participation. Their young people are naturally very adept at the robotic and hip-hop dances.

It's easy to see how the tonal graphs of the Germanic and romantic language cultures would lead to these different types of movements and dance styles. You could say that languages convey energy in motion, or emotion. The more flow to a language's melody, the more a culture tends to show emotion. From a business perspective, it's clear to see when looking at the tonal graphs that the Italian culture will typically have longer and more expressive conversations, with possibly more emotion as signified by the high and low tones, whereas the German culture will be more direct and to the point, with considerably less expression and emotion.

If you were to look at all the other existing languages on tonal graphs—such as the Asian, African, Oceanic, Middle Eastern, and

Slavic, to name a few—they would likely fall somewhere between the tonal graphs of the Germanic and romantic language cultures. It's not difficult to anticipate the amount of tonality and body language a culture will use if you know what the language sounds like. If a language has less melody and more hard sounds or words ending in consonants, chances are that culture will have less tonality and body language. If a language has more of these things, that culture is likely to have more tonality and body language.

I've often been asked where the English language falls on this continuum. Although English is a Germanic language, it is heavily influenced by the French language. Many English words even have the same spelling as the French words—such as those for table, orange, hotel, police, distraction, impression, and impossible—and are just pronounced differently.

Of course, there is a distinction between British, Canadian, Australian, Hindi, American, and other versions of English. I found out very quickly while living in Europe that British English is considered the purest form of the language. The words are fully pronounced, and there is less acceptable slang.

We also know that English is often spoken differently, even within the same country. For instance, in the United Kingdom, Scottish English and the Irish Brogue sound nothing like traditional Oxford English. There's a French influence on English on Canada's east coast and a British influence on the west coast. People in the Southern United States have *romanticized* English (given more *melody* to it) due both to the warmer climate and the Spanish influence, which resulted in the traditional Southern drawl. When languages are spoken differently or have different dialects, it also influences the business communication style. Since the Southern drawl is a more melodic or flowing version of English, the speakers tend to use more tonality and body language to accompany it. They also are apt to have more small talk in their business conversations, so discussions tend to be longer and more relaxed.

Where English lies on a tonal graph depends on the type of English being spoken. However, the melody and flow of the English language essentially falls somewhere in the middle between Germanic and romantic language cultures. The speech pattern curves for British English would likely fall slightly closer to the Germanic tonal graph, whereas those for the U.S. Southern drawl would likely fall slightly closer to the tonal graph of the romantic language cultures.

I've often told people that I'm damned if I do and damned if I don't when I travel internationally. In the Scandinavian countries, people can easily perceive me as being too warm and outgoing or exhibiting overly expressive tonality and body language. People from cultures like these frequently say that Americans wear their emotions like clothing. In contrast, if I go to the South American countries, people there may feel that I'm not warm and outgoing *enough* or that I don't use enough tonality and body language. I need to wear more "emotional clothing" for them.

However, because the English language falls somewhere in the middle of the tonal graphs, it's easier to adapt and add more or less tonality and body language as needed. It can be more challenging for cultures with very different language dynamics to adapt, because the differences are more pronounced.

The following is a list of cultures and how much melody is found in their languages and dialects; it begins with the ones that have the *least melody* in their languages, which means there is typically less expressive tonality and body language in their communication. The list progressively continues through the cultures that have the *most melody* in their language and consequently more expressive tonality and body language in their communication. Although this affects both business and social communication styles, obviously all cultures will tend to be more expressive in their social relationships than in business relationships.

Multicultural Language Dynamics

1. The Germanic, Scandinavian, and Nordic cultures

2. The Japanese culture

3. The Asian Pacific cultures

4. The English language cultures

5. The Russian, Eastern European, and Slavic cultures

6. The Middle East, Arabic, and North African cultures

7. The Latin or romantic language cultures

KEY THREE

Organize Productive Interactions

Understand Cultural Sensitivities and Avoid Conflict

The chapters in Key Three will cover what factors you need to consider when organizing cross-cultural interactions. Being successful in cross-cultural sales, in management, or when interacting with different cultures is directly related to your ability to grasp cultural sensitivities and avoid conflict. Failing to develop an awareness of how formality, hierarchy, and timing can affect business and decision making will thwart even the most seasoned professionals.

Because business interactions can often take longer in some cultures and countries than they do in others, you must plan accordingly. You want to avoid having people perceive you as overly aggressive or impatient—and to do so, you have to understand how various cultures relate to time. Are you "in time," "on time," or "out of time" with a particular culture?

E-mail has rapidly become the most commonly used method of business communication, with text next in line. We meet, greet, and establish relationships with e-mail; however, we have to appreciate the fact that once we put something in writing and send it, *it cannot be undone*. There, it's critical to learn how to avoid unintentionally offending someone from another culture via any form of written communication. It's important to be effective in all virtual communications, which are at the heart of global business and social exchanges.

Keep in mind as well that what works well for one culture won't necessarily work for another. Some cultures are more team-focused or we-oriented than others. This can clearly affect the business style and marketing material, including translations. You want to avoid having members of these cultures perceive you as too I-oriented or egocentric.

The following chapters will teach you how to effectively *frame your communication* for multicultural marketing, sales, management, and social interactions. This is essential to creating successful multicultural influencing and collaboration.

Multicultural Time Expectations

In Time, on Time, or out of Time?

The way in which different cultures relate to time can be a real challenge when you're trying to organize productive interactions between them. The first thing to keep in mind is that most countries outside the United States use the 24-hour clock (referred to as military time in the United States) instead of the 12-hour clock. For example, 7:00 PM would be written as 19:00. Another factor is that being in time, on time, or out of time doesn't mean the same to everyone—despite the fact that we all have the same 60 seconds in a minute, 60 minutes in an hour, 24 hours a day, and 365 days a year.

Time is like a bank. We are credited with 480 minutes in an 8-hour workday and 1,440 minutes in an entire 24-hour day each morning. And each night we write off as a loss what time we don't invest in good purpose. We can't carry any balance forward, and time allows for no overdraft.

So think about how you would feel if you received $480 (a dollar for every minute in an 8-hour workday) every morning—and lost every penny of the amount you had failed to use effectively every evening?

This loss is wholly yours. There is no going back or drawing against tomorrow. You must live on and invest in today's deposit to get the most out of life. When it comes to the time bank, *no one* wants to be in the red! Time is a gift—a valuable commodity, whether we are working or playing. How you use the gift of time determines how valuable it is to you.

Many of us are faced with the pressing question: What do we do about time robbers? We all know them. They say they will be someplace at a certain time and arrive late. They schedule events at a specific time, but then start late. They promise to complete a project by a particular time, and of course, they don't. We can excuse occasional delays; after all, they happen to all of us. But it's frustrating when this continually happens with specific people or cultures, and we can't seem to figure out why.

The most infamous, albeit unintentional, time robbers are probably those cultures that follow what is commonly known as Latin time. Most of us are aware that this means a time *later* than the stated time. It's received this name because Latin-based language cultures primarily created it. One of the biggest challenges we hear about in our cross-cultural classes has to do with cultural time differences, especially the differences with Latin time.

The difficulties with multicultural time differences really come down to how a particular culture defines *in time*. For example, *in time* to the Swiss culture means to be exactly *on* time. You certainly can't be late; however, they don't want you to arrive too early either. Anyone who's ever taken a train in Switzerland will notice that the trains roll in and out just as the second hand reaches the *exact* scheduled time—not a second before and not a second after. The land of Swiss watches is famous for being one of the most punctual countries in the world—a Swiss characteristic that generally holds true for the Swiss German, Swiss French, and Swiss Italian sections of the country. There may be a bit more time flexibility in the Swiss French and Swiss Italian sections, but they still operate on Swiss time.

You notice a fairly significant contrast if you take a look at what *in time* means to the Spanish culture. For this culture, it means something entirely different. Arriving somewhere "in time" is more flexible here. Arriving 15 to 30 minutes late is acceptably "on time." At the far end of the spectrum, it has even come to be known as *mañana*, which typically means "later" or "tomorrow morning." This kind of accommodating time frame applies, in varying degrees, to most all of the Latin language–based cultures, and it extends to both business and social interactions.

It's interesting to consider how this very loose definition of *on time* came to be for the Latin language–based cultures. To understand this, it helps to think about how a culture's environment can influence the behavioral styles of its people. One major factor at play here is that most Latin-based cultures are located in warmer climates. As we discussed in previous chapters, these cultures tend to be more relaxed and less rushed than colder climate cultures. For instance, they may encourage taking a nap or siesta after lunch, allowing for more flexibility in workday hours. Workdays tend to start later and extend until 7 or 8 PM to compensate for the leisurely midday meal and siesta. Overall, daily life in these cultures tends to be more relaxed, something that their relationship to time reflects.

This is why you'll find a more lenient approach to time in these warmer climate cultures, such as those in much of southern Europe, Latin and South America, Africa, the Middle East, the Oceanic and Island cultures, and those known to be vacation or resort destinations. Citizens of the Hawaiian Islands even have their own hand gesture to tell people, "Take it easy." They consider it impolite to honk your horn while driving in Hawaii. After all, what's the rush? They want to convey a message of, "Slow down and relax a bit." As a result, people in these cultures may also take a longer time to establish relationships, negotiate, and make decisions.

You can reduce frustration when working or interacting with people from the flexible time cultures by keeping in mind that being "on time" won't necessarily mean the *stated* time. The key is to ask *in advance* what *on time* means to the parties involved—and agree upon what the actual time is likely to be. For instance, if you know that you can plan on the actual time being 15 to 30 minutes later than the stated time, then you can make good use of those "extra" minutes. The actual time will still be on time, even though it differs from the stated time. It's simply a different time frame reference. And the most important part is that you won't be robbed of your time, because you can choose how to use it. However, it's advisable to be on time for *all* business—that is, *unless* you've made a prior agreement that the actual time will be 15 to 30 minutes later than the stated time.

The protocol for being on time in the workplace is determined by whether that workplace culture defines *in time* as *flexible* or *on time*. It is fairly easy in most cases to educate multicultural employees about how they should view time in a particular culture and work environment. As the multicultural business community is blending, time standards are becoming more uniform. As a result, the majority of global business cultures are more likely to be *on time* in their professional interactions.

It's crucial to keep in mind that both on time and flexible time cultures are in time according to *their* culture's reference. Successful cross-cultural interactions are about understanding and adhering to the time references of the cultures involved. When in Rome, do as the Romans—as long as it's agreed upon!

The following list shows some of the common cultures that tend to have *on time* or *flexible time* references. This list does not necessarily apply to all countries within the cultures. For example, Italy and Argentina expect punctuality for business meetings, and it is considered inappropriate not to let someone know if you will be late. Punctuality expectations are also different for business and social engagements, so although a culture may be punctual for business, it may be less punctual socially. Remember, whatever the situation, they are all in time:

On Time Cultures

- The Swiss cultures
- The Germanic, Scandinavian, and Nordic cultures
- The English-speaking cultures
- The Asia Pacific cultures
- The United Arab Emirates

Figure 13.1

Flexible Time Cultures

- The southern European cultures
- The Central and South American cultures
- The Middle Eastern and African cultures
- The Russian, Eastern European, and Slavic cultures
- Most tropical island cultures

Figure 13.2

E-Mail Etiquette Is Culturally Sensitive

Once It's Sent, It Cannot Be Undone

In today's global business environment, we frequently meet, greet, and establish relationships using virtual communication, especially e-mail. Very often, we never see or interact with the people with whom we have e-mail relationships in person. Sometimes, we don't even talk to them by phone because of the international time differences. Thanks to this, e-mail has firmly established its place as the number one method of business communication, and we use it almost as often for social relationships. And although we don't yet know the full impact that text and social media will have on business and social communication, it is safe to say that the cultural etiquette that is appropriate for e-mail would extend to text and social media as well.

E-mail is a relationship skill just like any other form of communication, and just as we would for an in-person or telephone relationship, we need to establish the terms up front. However, e-mail comes with one unique characteristic that other communication methods don't share: *Once something has been put in writing and sent via e-mail, it cannot be undone.* If you offend someone in an e-mail, the recipient can read it over and over again—and the person usually feels worse with each subsequent reading. Whereas with interpersonal or phone conversations, each person has their own recollection of what was said, which is open to perceptual differences—unless you have left a voice message, which like e-mail, cannot be undone.

It's also important to keep in mind that all e-mail has a permanent record *somewhere* and that today's technology has no problem finding it. E-mail evidence has been responsible for many lawsuits relating to cultural diversity and regulatory violations.

So be *extremely* careful and give careful thought about what you put in writing. You want to make sure, as best you can, that it does not cause miscommunication and misunderstanding. Avoid all jokes specific to a race, gender, or culture. Be mindful that USING ALL CAPS is considered yelling to many people. Avoid the overuse of bold, color, and the exclamation point for "important" e-mails. If you send every e-mail with "high priority," people won't treat the *truly* high-priority e-mail as such; they'll simply dismiss it as one of your regular messages. And because everyone has a different idea of what is important, ask yourself if the receiver of your e-mail will consider it as important as you do.

When it comes to e-mail, it's best to model the sender, which is especially the case for multicultural e-mail. E-mail etiquette or "netiquette"—like most written communication—is culturally sensitive. Therefore, one of the safest ways to avoid offending someone with an e-mail is to model the *format* someone uses to e-mail you.

In general, the Asian Pacific, Indian, southern European, Middle Eastern, and Latin American cultures are *more formal* in their e-mail and written communication than other cultures. Politeness is important to these individuals, so they may start an e-mail with "Dear" and will usually add some courteous small talk at the beginning. They tend to close with "Kind regards" or even "Warm regards." They are more likely to use surnames and professional titles. If they're e-mailing someone for the first time, they normally like to give an "e-mail handshake"— a warm, personal introduction. They are expressive, tending to use descriptive adjectives and adverbs and generally staying away from abbreviations (such as *re:* for "regarding"). They may say, "Thank you," whether there is anything specifically to thank someone for or not. And because the e-mails with these cultures are more formal, they are also inclined to be longer.

The most formal e-mail I ever received was from the president of a South American country. Mind you, it was several years ago, and things were generally more formal at that time. However, given the nature of the e-mail and the person who sent it, it would probably look pretty much the same today. It went something like this:

> *My Dear Madame, Gayle Cotton, President of Circles Of Excellence,*
> *It is with sincere pleasure that I humbly request that you, and members of your staff, come to our country to work with my staff and me on our presentations skills for our upcoming negotiations with Israel and China. We would like to be culturally sensitive and as polished as possible. We would be honored to have you help us with the following things* . . . (The e-mail continued to go on with great detail!)
> *I send my kindest regards,*

As you can see, this e-mail was extremely formal. I seriously doubt that we would have gotten the contract to work with him had I sent a less formal e-mail like this:

> *Dear President* _____,
> *Our current available dates are* . . .
> *Sincerely,*

I needed to reply as graciously as I was invited. My responding e-mail looked more like this:

> *Dear President* _____,
> *It was very much an honor to receive your e-mail requesting our company's assistance with your presentation skills for the negotiations with Israel and China. It would be a great pleasure to come to your country to work with you and you staff* . . .
> *Most sincerely,*

I must have done something right—because after three months of developing our relationship via e-mail, we got the contract. And our e-mails became progressively less formal as we continued to communicate back and forth. Just prior to our trip, the president sent a typical e-mail request. Because the Spanish language has a formal and informal version of the word *you,* he wanted to take the step toward using the informal version, which usually also signals a move toward using first names.

That e-mail started something like this:

Dear Madame Cotton,
Since we will be working so intimately together, may I invite you to
call me by my first name, _____?

Of course, that was my signal to invite him to call me by my first name as well. In these situations, it is usually the highest-ranking or elder individual who initially extends the first name invitation. I couldn't help but laugh a little when I read his e-mail because of his use of the word *intimately*. Although this is a common use of the word in many of the Latin American countries, the connotation is a bit different in the United States! When I showed my husband the e-mail, his apprehensive response was, *"Who exactly are you going to work with?"* Needless to say, these e-mails have earned a permanent place in my e-mail files!

As a rule, U.S., British, Canadian, Australian, and northern European cultures are *more direct* and to the point in both their e-mail and written communications. Although polite, they are usually less formal. They are less inclined to start their e-mails with "Dear," generally using first names and making professional titles somewhat optional (with the exception of "Dr."). Their e-mails are well organized with little, if any, small talk at the beginning. There is less descriptive use of adjectives and adverbs, in favor of clarity and simplicity. They believe that it's appropriate to use abbreviations such as *re:* as long as everyone understands what they mean and tend to say "Thank you" only when they're thanking someone for something specific. Their closing is more likely to be "Best regards" or simply "Regards," and their e-mails tend to be more precise, focused, and, as a result, shorter. (Note: These guidelines don't necessarily apply to the Canadian Province of Quebec. Since they are French Canadian, they may follow a more formal protocol.)

As result of blending these various multicultural styles, e-mail is becoming more direct and less conversational from a global perspective. The brief nature of text communication has also had a great influence on e-mail. As with interpersonal and phone communication, e-mail—and really, all written communication—is evolving as cultures blend. Nevertheless, we need to be mindful of the protocol for multicultural e-mail.

Because I travel frequently for business, I constantly remind myself to pay attention and change my e-mail style for the country in which I'm currently working. After living in the United States for several years, my personal e-mail style has become quite direct and to the point. I'm very comfortable using first names, getting to the point, and using abbreviations, and my closing is typically "Best regards."

Several years ago when I was working in the Swiss French culture of Geneva, Switzerland, I e-mailed someone to confirm a meeting that we'd previously scheduled by phone. I sent the e-mail without using "Dear" or the surname "Monsieur." I didn't open with any polite small talk, and I confirmed the meeting using the abbreviation *re:*. I also neglected to say, "Thank you," because it was a simple e-mail confirmation, and I didn't think it was necessary. My closing was my standard "Best regards." After sending, I was promptly informed by someone in our office that "I needed more *butter* on my e-mail." When I asked what *that* meant, I was told that I had sent a "dry piece of bread," meaning that my e-mail needed something to make it more appetizing. (I guess the French really *do* think in terms of food much of the time!)

A more appropriate (and appealing) e-mail would have been the following:

Dear Monsieur _____,
It was a pleasure talking with you this morning. I am happy to be able to confirm our meeting this Friday afternoon at 3:00 P.M.
I look forward to meeting with you.
Thank you for your time.
Kind regards,

I've never forgotten that lesson. E-mail is the most important form of business communication we currently have. It is as important of a relationship skill as our interpersonal and phone communication.

The following 10 golden rules of e-mail should be the guidelines for all cross-cultural e-mails.

10 Golden Rules of E-Mail

1. When possible, model the e-mail sender's style and format. Use their surname and title if they use it in introductions or e-mails. If you are the first one to e-mail someone from another culture, follow the guidelines for formality. When in doubt, err on the side of formality.

2. If e-mailing someone new for the first time, give the person an "e-mail handshake" with a personal introduction. Use a little polite conversation to establish rapport.

3. Have a clear, specific subject line that identifies the e-mail's purpose.

4. Avoid the overuse of all capital letters, color, and bold. *Italics* are preferable for emphasis.

5. Organize your e-mail with priorities and discuss the most important things first. People frequently don't read to the very end of e-mails.

6. Put all related information together, possibly into categories, for clarity.

7. Use bullets or numbers for distinction of "points of attention."

8. Ask the receiver of the e-mail to let you know if he or she has any questions.

9. Copy or reply to only related parties. Be careful of the icons for Copy All or Reply to All. Almost everyone has had the unfortunate experience of copying or replying to the wrong people!

10. Make sure to include your contact information and to choose the best closing phrase for the culture of the person you are e-mailing.

CHAPTER
15

Triple Cross-Translate

Who Wrote These Instructions?

Although multicultural written communication can be challenging, it's nothing compared with the challenge of achieving effective verbal translation. There is nothing worse than having something poorly translated into another language.

Not long ago, I referred to an instruction manual for how to change a battery on a technical device. The battery section had one of the most hilarious translations I've ever seen. It was so funny that I read the entire manual and couldn't believe what I was reading! I would love to know how they came up with that translation. We now use those instructions as an example of how *not* to translate in all of our cross-cultural training courses.

The translation for what the instruction manual says about batteries is as follows.

Caution in Using Battery

Do not use in driving and walking since any accident could be happened. Do not have a short circuit, disassemble, heat or put battery in the fire, and do harm to eyes, also could cause the rupture of a doctor!

This is where you ask yourself—as I did—"*Who* wrote those instructions?"

Figure 15.1

Perhaps the most disappointing part is that the company responsible for the translation is a well-known technology company. How embarrassing for them to have this example of poor translation distributed all over the world.

This isn't the first time that we have seen translations this inaccurate—nor will it be the last. It happens more frequently than one might think. This battery example just happens to be one of the most humorous we've seen. When I really need a good laugh, I still pick up that instruction manual!

Of course, it's difficult to get an absolutely perfect translation; however, you can take some precautions to ensure that they are as accurate as possible. One way to ensure greater accuracy is to triple cross-translate. This requires a *minimum* of three cross-translations, using three highly qualified, expert translators.

How to Triple Cross-Translate

1. The initial translator does the initial translation, known as the first version, or V1.

2. A second translator does a cross-translation between the original material and the first translator's translation of the material. This person either agrees with the first translator's interpretation or suggests changes and modifications to create a second version—V2.

3. If the second translator suggests modifications, the first and second translators compare and evaluate the two versions. They then

agree on one of the two versions or come up with a third version—V3—to submit to a third translator.

4. The third translator does the final cross-translation based on a review and comparison between the original material and the translation they received. This third translator either agrees with the interpretation of the previous translators or recommends the changes and modifications he or she feels are needed to fully capture the original material's meaning. This becomes the fourth version—or V4.

5. All three translators then compare and agree on V4 as being the most accurate or come up with a fifth version—V5—which is the final version used.

Triple cross-translation should ensure that the translation is basically accurate. However, additional cross-translations may be necessary for high-profile translations, global distributions, and those with many nuances or technical jargon.

I've worked with quite a few translators and interpreters during my career as a professional speaker. It can be challenging—and occasionally disastrous—if their interpretation doesn't convey the message you intend to get across. It becomes even *more* challenging when a simultaneous translation is being done through headphones—because you don't know what the audience is hearing.

I was involved in a particularly challenging translation experience many years ago, just after the Berlin Wall came down. I had completed a video production about business and free enterprise in Ostrava, the Czech Republic (which was still Czechoslovakia at that time). The presentation was going to be translated from English into Czech and various other languages for the Eastern European countries. However, since these countries had been under communist control for more than 40 years, *there were no words for anything related to business and free enterprise in Czech*—or in any of the other languages. Our translators had to go back to dictionaries from nearly 50 years prior to find out what these words used to be in the various languages.

As a result, we had to postpone the video production for three months to give the translators time to merely *find the words* they needed to express what the videos were about. We also had to create a *Word Guide* to accompany the videos to ensure that the viewers would be able to understand the words that we were using—*in their own languages!*

Of course, not all translation scenarios will be this extreme. However, when you're in a situation in which it's necessary to work with interpreters, the following guidelines are helpful.

Guidelines for Working with Interpreters

- Send the material to be translated to the interpreter in advance. When possible, have the person translate the material and then send it back so an independent cross-translation may be done.

- Keep in mind that a presentation with direct translation (where the interpreter speaks immediately after you speak) will typically double the time of the presentation.

- Introduce the interpreter to your audience (be it an audience of one or 100), and describe your respective roles to clarify the expectations. (Keep in mind that an introduction isn't always possible if the interpreter is doing a simultaneous translation through headphones in a sequestered area.)

- During the presentation, address the person or group you are speaking to, *not* the interpreter. Do the same for any remarks, questions, and answers.

- Limit what you say, as well as remarks, questions, and answers from the audience, to a few sentences between the translations.

- Pause after you speak a few sentences to signal the interpreter to begin the translation.

- Give clear and concise explanations that easily convey what the audience needs to understand. However, be careful not to *over*simplify.

- Give instructions in a clear and logical sequence. Emphasize the key words or points, and offer reasons for any specific recommendations.

- Observe your audience's nonverbal communication to make sure they understand the translation. If necessary, ask the interpreter to clarify.

- Periodically check your audience's comprehension and the translation's accuracy. Have the interpreter ask if there are any specific questions about what has been translated. But avoid literally asking, "Do you understand?" because this may make the audience members less inclined to answer.

- Avoid giving too much or overly complex information at one time.

- Avoid technical jargon, colloquialisms, idioms, slang, analogies, and anything that doesn't translate well.

- When possible, reinforce the verbal information with materials written in the audience's language. To assist in comprehension, use visual aids when possible.

- Keep in mind that when addressing multicultural audiences, a picture is worth a thousand words!

chapter 16

It Takes Two to Collaborate

How to Position and Influence

It's no secret that collaboration takes (at least) two; indeed, it is the basis for all interpersonal connections. It requires cooperation and working *jointly* to achieve a mutual goal or outcome. We influence and collaborate with others in nearly everything we do, both for business and social interactions.

The essential nature of influencing and collaboration involves two basic components or tendencies:

1. Our inner driving needs and what people want
2. Our inner concerns and what people fear or don't want

The first of these factors is *aspirational.* In other words, it is linked to what we *want* for ourselves and for those important to us. It involves our goals and objectives. Therefore, we will seek to exert a positive influence in order to achieve these goals. We accept others' influence when it is consistent with these goals. The concept of aspirational influence is also referred to as moving toward the carrot—or making our way toward what we want.

The second of these factors is *protective*—linked to what we want to *avoid or minimize* for ourselves and those important to us. Therefore, we will seek to exert a negative influence to avoid an outcome we don't want. We resist others' influence when it may lead to unwanted outcomes. The concept of protective influence is also referred to as moving away from the stick—in the opposite direction of what we *don't* want.

Everyone is familiar with the Golden Rule: "Do to others as you would have them do to you." However, this doesn't always make sense in terms of influencing. It would indicate that every individual likes to be influenced in the same way as we do, which is clearly not the case, especially when we're interacting with people from other cultures.

For example, some groups—such as the Germanic and English language cultures—prefer a fast-paced, factual, *outcome-oriented* influencing style that results in quicker decision making. Others—such as Asian and Latin language cultures—prefer a slower-paced, conceptual, *process-oriented* influencing style that results in decisions taking longer to make.

The concept of collaboration means something unique to every culture, and every country's expectations are different. When influencing multiculturally, it is sometimes necessary to adapt and "walk in the other person's shoes." Trying to influence a person *the way you like to be influenced* won't always get the results you want. Being empathetic—and showing that you can understand how the other person sees the world—will go a long way toward success. Failing to do so risks aggravating, annoying, and inciting anger—because you're assuming that another person is comfortable with the same approach as you are. Your best approach is to get on the same wavelength and not push the wrong buttons, which will help you effectively influence and collaborate.

A few years ago, I was shopping for a ring at the gold souk in Dubai, UAE, a place that definitely puts one's bargaining skills of collaboration, influencing, and negotiations to the test. As I walked through the souk, I saw merchants positioning their wares with the utmost finesse, trying to influence me to make my purchase from them. As I listened to their various presentations, I realized that, as a patron, I needed to select the merchant with whom I could best *collaborate* to find exactly what I was looking for, with the quality I wanted, and at a reasonable price. It wasn't about buying and selling; it was about collaboration.

I began to engage with various merchants in a *collaborative approach*. I told them that I was looking for the best "partner" to help me find a specific style of ring, of a particular quality, and within a certain price range. I wasn't interested in looking at anything that didn't fit my needs. I wanted to work jointly with them *to help them help me*. To do that, we needed to explore the possibility that they might have what I was looking for. That is where the journey began. Instead of them showing *all* the rings they wanted to sell to me, it became about me describing to them what I wanted to buy. In essence, *I was helping them influence me by influencing them*. Some merchants were very good at this collaboration and partnership with me. They definitely did their best, whether they were able to satisfy my needs or not. Others were stuck in the process of selling me on a ring that was completely wrong and never got beyond it.

The merchant from whom I ended up buying actually didn't have a ring with the style, quality, and price I wanted; however, he understood very well what I needed. He asked me if I could come back the next day and said that he would have the perfect ring for me if I did. Although I rather doubted this would be the case, I returned the next day as he suggested. To my surprise, he *had* found the perfect ring for me! I didn't even have to barter for it, because I'd already made clear the price I expected and was willing to pay. And when I had an independent jeweler appraise the ring, he agreed that the price was more than fair.

Collaboration is about cooperation. To be effective, it needs to be as win-win as possible. The objective should have a *mutual benefit* that both parties are willing to work toward achieving. Collaboration is the precursor to any type of effective negotiation. Instead of working as separate parties on opposing sides, people must be on the *same side* for the purpose of achieving the common goal or outcome. Collaboration should also be focused on *asking*, rather than telling. Questions will help determine the needs of the parties involved. It's crucial to have *reciprocal*, or two-way, discussions to uncover the best ways to achieve the objective. Challenges arrive when important issues are concealed or avoided and when the parties involved begin to compete with one another. The doors to collaboration remain open when you instead choose to accommodate or compromise as necessary.

The following guidelines will help in the collaborative process.

10 Guidelines to Effective Collaboration

1. Adapt your verbal and nonverbal communication for cross-cultural rapport.
2. Allow enough time for understanding in non–mother tongue languages. It can take up to 50 percent longer to communicate when there are language differences.
3. Know whether you will be collaborating with an individual or a team of individuals.
4. Keep the communication reciprocal; make sure there is a two-way conversation.
5. Clearly define the collaboration's goal or the objective.
6. Start with a creative problem-solving approach, and keep it as simple as possible.
7. Explore all uncertainties, concerns, or objections of the parties involved.
8. Create options and solutions that will work well for all concerned.
9. Agree to act on the best option or solution.
10. Keep it as win-win as possible for mutual benefit.

It is also important to note during these kinds of multicultural collaborations that some cultures are more team-oriented than others. They are known as the *we* cultures—the ones you will likely hear say, "*We* can do it." If an individual is given a compliment, they are likely to *credit everyone* involved by emphasizing that, "It was a *team effort.*" Other cultures can sometimes view people like this as lacking individual confidence. It has even resulted in some team-oriented individuals being bypassed for promotion, because they promoted their team instead of themselves and their ability. *Team-oriented cultures work as a group for the good of the group.* Many of the Asian and Latin language cultures fall into this category.

When you meet with team-oriented cultures, you'll typically encounter a group of individuals rather than just one person. Usually their teams are organized with specific representation from the corporate hierarchy or with professionals of a particular expertise. It's important to choose a similar group of individuals to meet with them. For example, if they will have very senior levels present, make sure that you are represented by equal levels of seniority. Choosing a lower level of seniority would convey to this other group that the meeting isn't as important to you as it is to them. Because they will communicate using the word *we*, avoid overusing the word *I*, lest they see you as egocentric. When team cultures collaborate, influence, or negotiate, it is done *as a team, for the team.*

We recently helped a multinational consulting company launch a large project in the team-oriented country of China. Chinese professionals generally meet and negotiate with teams and consider the team hierarchy to be very important. True collaboration is the goal, so everything needs to be as win-win as possible.

The project had four phases, each of which depended on the prior phase to succeed. It was therefore essential that the first phase work in order for the next three to pan out as well. We spent months collaborating with our customer to ensure that we fully understood the full scope of the project. We wanted to be able to position them in the best possible way for all four phases, which were:

1. The marketing material
2. The sale
3. The on-site consultancy
4. The presentation of results

We started with the first step and made sure that everything was team- or we-oriented. To that end, nothing in the marketing material could be interpreted as egocentric. Rather than it asking, "What can *I* do for *you?*" it inquired, "How can *we* help *your team?*" In addition, we selected a design with appropriate colors for the marketing materials with the Chinese culture in mind. It's important to research color choices when marketing to different countries and cultures.

Once this phase was complete, we trained the sales team that was travelling to China. They were carefully educated about the Chinese ways, taught the preferred communication style, and instructed in the Chinese business protocol. Because they were coming from the United States—a more individual-oriented culture—we made sure to prepare them well for China's team-oriented customs. Relationships with the Chinese can take considerable time to develop, and negotiations take longer; therefore, it was necessary for the sales team to make several trips to China—and work for more than a year before finalizing the sale. Patience is a virtue in China!

The consultancy phase was even more challenging than the sales phase. Our U.S. consultants would be living in China for three to six months to gather the necessary information. They needed to be able to communicate with the assistance of an interpreter, maintain rapport, assess the business systems, evaluate their findings, and gain the cooperation of the Chinese in the workplace. They had to be very deliberately collaborative in all their efforts and communications. Not once could they say, "*I* am here to find out," or "*I* am here to help *you*." They had to remember to present things as, "*We* are here to find out," or "*We* are here to help *the Chinese team*." They were there to *partner* with and form a *team* with the Chinese in order to gain the respect and help they needed for their analysis.

The presentation of results was probably the most challenging phase of all. The consultants were going to return to China to present the results of their assessment. That required telling the Chinese how to improve what they were currently doing—*without the Chinese losing face*. This is not an easy thing to do. Losing face is similar to an insult, where the reputation of an individual or group is tarnished, or reduced, in the eyes of peers. Not only is it important to avoid this, but the consultants must be able to *save face* when necessary, or even *give face* when possible. Giving face improves the "good face" or reputation that an individual or group currently has. Having "face" is one of the most important concepts in China. It is directly linked to Guanxi (gwahn-shee), an individual's or group's collective network of relationships or circle of influence.

Accomplishing this final phase required that the consultants use their best collaborative skills. By praising what the Chinese company currently had in place (giving face) and then linking it to the recommendations that would make the Chinese company *even* better (again, giving face), the consultants were able to present their findings *and* get buy-in for their recommended changes. The effective collaboration between an individual- and a team-oriented culture had created success in all four phases or the project.

Following are some cultures that tend to be more team-oriented.

Team-Oriented Cultures

- The Asian Pacific cultures
- The Central and South American cultures

- The southern European cultures
- The Russian, Eastern European, and Slavic cultures
- The Middle Eastern and northern/sub-Saharan African cultures
- Most tropical island cultures

Following are some cultures that tend to be more individual-oriented.

Individual-Oriented Cultures

- The English-speaking cultures
- The Germanic language cultures
- The Scandinavian and Nordic cultures
- The northern European cultures

Members of these "I" cultures are the ones you'll hear say, "I can do it!" They are happy to take *individual credit* for a job well done. They don't hesitate to position themselves for promotion, which works well in their own culture but not as well in team-oriented cultures. Meeting one on one is expected and perfectly acceptable when collaborating, influencing, or negotiating with these cultures.

Some cultures, due to various environmental and language factors, can be either team- or individual-oriented. For example, in Switzerland, the Swiss German culture may be more independent-oriented, whereas the Swiss Italian culture is more team-oriented. It's important to find out the expectations and protocol in advance with mid-range cultures.

Following are some cultures that tend to be more mid-range cultures.

Mid-Range Cultures

- The French-speaking cultures, including French Canada
- The Swiss cultures
- The Belgian culture
- The Israeli culture
- The cultures of India
- The South African culture
- The United Arab Emirates

Even though cultural homogenization is causing cultures to integrate their collaborative styles, the team orientation or individual orientation preferences are still firmly in place in many cultures.

The most important thing to remember is that all persuasion, influencing, and negotiation skills are based on the ability to collaborate—and that collaboration always takes two, three, four, or more!

CHAPTER

17

Framing Your Cross-Cultural Communication

For Sales, Negotiations, Management, and International Travel

Communication framing is one of the most important tools we have to use in both business and social multicultural interactions. It *organizes* the communication process to make it as simple, clear, and as easy to understand as possible. It's necessary to think about the best way to communicate very important or complicated topics so that people will receive the message as it's intended. We always want to communicate with the intended receiver in mind, especially in cross-cultural communication.

We must think about what a particular person needs to hear to best understand the message and about the most effective way to convey it to that person—given his or her culture and level of knowledge. This is essential to effectively lead and manage multicultural workforces. If our company coaches executives and they aren't using communication framing, it is the first thing we recommend.

Every culture has its own sensitivities. But no matter what they are, communication framing helps people avoid unintentionally offending others or pushing the wrong buttons. When possible, it's always best to eliminate conflict *before* it starts.

Communication framing is a critical part of multicultural sales and negotiations; it can even turn "no chance for a sale" into a "potential future sale." We recently helped a European company prepare for an important multinational negotiation for which the previous round had not gone well. We spent four days teaching executives the best negotiation approach for the various multinationals involved. We had them rehearse their negotiation frames, overcome objections, and rehearse again, until we were confident that they were prepared to close the deal. The specifics on how to effectively frame your communication for negotiations, or other important interactions, will be discussed later in this chapter.

Success in sales and negotiations depends entirely on how you *position* your expectations. You need to *think* like the customer; when you view the situation from the customer's perspective, you become *benefit-oriented*, which is key. You need to answer from the customer's point of view, "Why should I care about this? What can you do for me?" Whenever possible, you want to anticipate the customer's questions, concerns, and objections *in advance*. After all, if you can eliminate your customer's doubts by addressing them before they even come up, then your customer will have much less to protest!

After our team had spent a few weeks working with this European company, we received a letter from the client's director of global sales. The letter was very complimentary, but the following section was what stood out the most:

> *We were behind closed doors for four straight hours with no break [during our recent negotiations]. I can't remember everything we learned in your course, but I do remember the communication frames. We used the pre-frame, reframe, agreement frame, and the feedback frame over and over again. The agreement frame kept the lines of communication open, when I was sure the doors would close. I want to thank you for your inspired and knowledgeable approach in helping us close the largest contract in our history.*

The concept of communication framing can be likened to the process of assembling a jigsaw puzzle when you don't know what the puzzle picture looks like. If you don't know your objective, it is very challenging to do—even more so when the pieces are upside down or if there are no colors to give it context. The correlation to communication framing is that it's very difficult to communicate if you haven't identified the big picture or objective of the communication. And it's even more challenging when you can't relate what is being communicated in a context that is meaningful to you.

We ask attendees in our cross-cultural courses how they would put together a jigsaw puzzle if all the pieces were *upside down* on a table and the only thing they saw was the gray cardboard backs of the puzzle pieces. They have no puzzle box showing a picture, so they have *no idea what the puzzle was.* It could be a puzzle of a Japanese tea garden or a safari in Kenya.

After thinking about it for a bit, attendees tend to say that they'll start by putting together the puzzle corners, since these are likely the easiest pieces to match up. Next, they would assemble the sides, creating the outside *frame* to provide a size and boundaries—and something to which they can connect the pieces. Next, they would begin to match up related pieces until they had several chunks of the puzzle assembled. They would then fit the chunks together into the frame of the puzzle until complete.

Although this is a very logical approach, it's also a rather difficult way to assemble a puzzle. After all, it's much easier when you know what the final puzzle picture looks like!

One of the most pressing challenges in the communication process—especially in multicultural interactions—is an inability to effectively convey the big picture or communication objective. Because our minds can think faster than we can effectively convey our words, this is not an uncommon occurrence. Instead of giving a brief overview of the discussion's purpose, we often jump right into the details. As a result, the person to whom we are talking gets lost in the details before really comprehending the underlying point. And without an understanding of where this dialogue is going, it's very difficult to follow. It can create confusion, misunderstanding, jumping to conclusions, objections, and worst of all, conflict.

Communication framing *organizes* this process to help avoid these very things. It is especially useful for important or complicated topics, where you need to think about the best way to frame what you want to say—and for the person to whom you want to say it. Most of us have heard someone say something like, "That was framed very well," meaning that we think they communicated their point effectively.

We've probably also heard the opposite, "That wasn't framed very well," implying that something could have been said more clearly.

Even when something isn't framed well and conflict does arise, communication framing can be useful. It helps restore the exchange to a more productive level and ensures a positive outcome.

There are four basic communication frames that correlate to a puzzle's four corners. They are the cornerstones or anchor points of what is being communicated, and they ultimately become the frame for the dialogue's objective.

You can then attach any related information—or *chunks of communication*—to the frame. This works the same way as fitting a chunk of puzzle pieces into a puzzle's frame, in that you will be able to figure out rather quickly whether it fits or not. If it does, all is understood and the communication can continue. If it doesn't, you must either clarify what you're saying or replace it with something that fits better.

The chunking keeps everyone focused on one portion until you're ready to add the next one. Eventually, you have a *series of chunks* that everyone can agree with. This fits into the overall objective of the conversation, just like the frame of a puzzle. It also enhances all the involved parties' memory of what has been discussed. It is much easier to remember a series of chunks—agreed-upon information—than a random bunch of details that have no organization.

Communication framing also creates checkpoints of understanding along the way. When you organize your communication *in advance* according to the four frames, you significantly reduce the likelihood of confusion and misunderstanding.

The first communication frame is the preframe. We can compare this to the process of framing a house under construction. Clearly, this border is essential to defining the home's architecture and room definition. If a room is missing, or if its size isn't correct, the house will need to be *reframed*.

1. The Preframe

- Its goal is to convey the big picture, or the point of the communication, in the clearest, most concise way possible. It requires some advance thought to determine the best way to do this to achieve optimal results.

- It *sets the stage* for what you want the message's receiver to *focus on* or perceive.

- It creates the expectations for the conversation's goal or objective.
- It positions the message in the most effective way for the person or group for whom the message is intended.
- It needs to incorporate the appropriate verbal and nonverbal communication styles for the cultures involved.
- It establishes the credibility and congruency of the person doing the preframe.
- It often connects what is unknown or unfamiliar to something that is known or familiar.
- It is usually benefit-oriented when used in sales and negotiations. If possible, it should also answer any questions, concerns, and objections *in advance*.
- *An effective preframe will eliminate the need for a reframe.*

Example:

The purpose of this conversation is to establish the necessary procedures for launching the Acclimate project in Geneva, southwestern France, northern Italy, and Poland.

The second communication frame is the reframe, which is used when the preframe wasn't clear, wasn't complete, or contained an element of inaccuracy (like a house that was framed with a room missing or that had a room that wasn't the right size).

2. The Reframe

- The reframe *clarifies*, completes, or corrects something in the preframe.
- It is the message sender's responsibility.
- It changes what the message's receiver should be focusing on or alters the receiver's *perception* to align better with the sender's intention.
- It recreates the expectations for the conversation's goal or objective.
- It repositions the message *in a more* effective way *for the receiver*.
- If necessary, it reestablishes the credibility and congruency of the message's sender.

- It corrects any misunderstanding or miscommunication.
- It explains any misinterpretations resulting from verbal or non-verbal language.
- In sales and negotiations, it restates or adds to the benefits and readdresses any remaining uncertainties, questions, concerns, or objections.
- *Reframes can continue until all parties involved understand the point of the communication.*

Example:

I didn't communicate that as well as I could have. Please allow me to clarify that when I said southwestern France, I meant to include Toulouse as well.

The third communication frame is the agreement frame, also known as the greatest conflict resolution tool. When overcoming challenges, the agreement frame helps keep the doors of communication open by empathizing with the message's intended receiver.

3. The Agreement Frame

- It *acknowledges* another person's opinion, concerns, or objections.
- It doesn't necessarily imply that you agree with this person; it simply means that you acknowledge the person's right to think and feel a certain way.
- It should use *neutral language* and keep the lines of communication open.
- It helps overcome any angry or upset feelings and returns the conversation to a more productive exchange.
- To be effective, it must avoid putting anyone on the defensive. *If someone is pushed, that person will likely push back—which defeats the purpose of the agreement frame.*
- It creates a channel for constructive feedback and eliminates destructive feedback.
- When possible, it seeks to eliminate conflict *before* it starts.
- It creates understanding when there has been a misunderstanding.

- It presents alternatives and options when disagreement arises.
- *Agreement frames work toward a solution or compromise that all concerned can accept.*

Example:

I agree that it may not be comfortable with Paolo along for the whole trip and unfortunately we aren't able to have Jean Pierre accompany us the entire time; however, *it might be possible to have Heinrich replace Paolo when we go to Poland.*

Note: When using the agreement frame in the English language, it's best to avoid the word *but* as a connector word. Although *but* or *mais* works very well in French and some other languages, it has a negative connotation in English because of its overuse. You may have even heard someone say, "Okay, where's the 'but'?"—which implies that something negative is inevitably coming. It is more effective within the agreement frame to use the words *however, and,* or *yet.* You can also simply pause and use no connector word at all. Whatever connector word you choose to use, it's important to keep your tone of voice *conversational* and not overly emphasize the word by saying, "*How . . . e . . . ver.*" Keep this in mind: *But builds walls instead of bridges.*

The fourth communication frame is the feedback frame. This confirms that the parties involved understand the conversation—something that's crucial to do with cross-cultural language differences.

4. The Feedback Frame

- It uses questions to confirm what the involved parties have understood (or misunderstood) over the course of a conversation.
- Most often, it uses closed or yes/no questions to elicit the necessary feedback.
- Typically, it asks three questions to confirm understanding of the most important points. Three confirmations of understanding will usually verify that the people involved have comprehended the exchange as intended; however, you may ask more questions if necessary.
- It can be used after *any of the previous frames* to confirm that everyone has understood the same thing in the conversation. Like a

reflective question, which reflects your understanding of what has been said, it can be used at any time in the communication process. Sometimes a good preframe and feedback frame are all that are needed!

- It can also be used to confirm what actions or next steps need to be taken.

- *The feedback frame is especially important in multicultural communications to confirm that the message has been understood as intended.*

Example:

1. You are planning to send the order October 15, correct? . . . "Yes."
2. The order will confirm the shipping address we'll need? . . . "Yes."
3. The managers of both divisions have approved the order? . . . **"No."**

(If the answer is, "No," it is necessary to clarify what has been understood.)

Note: Members of some cultures are hesitant to say, "No," directly, because it's considered impolite in certain countries and/or regions. Many of the Asian, southern European, and Latin American cultures fall into this category. In scenarios involving these cultures, we recommend using a descriptive feedback frame rather than the traditional feedback frame. This frame uses open or who, what, when, where, why, and how questions to elicit feedback, which avoids putting someone in the position of having to answer "No" directly.

5. The Descriptive Feedback Frame

Example:

1. When are you planning to send the order? . . . "October 15."
2. How will the shipping address be confirmed? . . . "It will be confirmed with the order."
3. Who are the two managers who have approved the order? . . . **"One manager, Jim Smith, has approved the order."**

If the answer is different than you expected, it is necessary to clarify what has been understood.

You can determine whether communication framing is successful based on what happens between the exchange's sender and receiver. Countless factors influence how communication will be received, but it always starts with the sender. This individual has a thought or topic in mind he or she intends to communicate. When communicating that to the receiver, the individual is, in essence, encoding a message. That encoding is based on several factors that affect the message's outcome.

The receiver then decodes this message and forms his or her own conclusion about what the sender has communicated. That decoding is also based on several factors that affect the message's outcome.

The receiver then provides feedback to the sender or encodes a message in response. His or her response determines whether the sender's message has been understood as expected or if further clarification is needed. There has either been effective communication or miscommunication.

Factors That Affect the Sender's Message

- The sender's communication style and how skilled a communicator the person is.
- How much experience and/or knowledge the sender has with both the topic being communicated and different communication styles.
- The depth of knowledge the sender has about the topic.
- Whether the sender is speaking in his or her native language or in a second or third language.
- The sender's social and cultural awareness or natural social tendencies and behavioral dynamics.
- The sender's attitude at the time of communication. Is the sender in a resourceful or nonresourceful state of mind at the time? This person's attitude can definitely have an impact on how the communication is received. In other words, "What side of the bed did the sender get up on?"
- How well prepared the sender is to communicate the message. The sender may have excellent communication skills, experience, knowledge, multilingual skills, sociocultural awareness, and a great attitude; however, if the person is unprepared to communicate the thought or topic, the messages won't be received as intended.

Factors That Affect How a Message Is Received

- The receiver's communication style and how skilled he or she is as a communicator.

- How much experience and/or knowledge the receiver has with both the topic being communicated and with different communication styles.

- The depth of knowledge the receiver has about the topic.

- Whether the receiver is speaking in his or her native language or in a second or third language.

- The receiver's social and cultural awareness.

- The receiver's attitude at the time of communication. Same question as with the sender: "What side of the bed did the receiver get up on?"

- Whether the receiver is prepared to receive the message or to receive the message *at that time.* Even someone with the best communication skills, experience, knowledge, multilingual skills, sociocultural awareness, and great attitude won't understand or accept a message well if he or she isn't prepared to receive it.

Table 17.1 illustrates what happens between the sender and receiver in communication.

The important thing to keep in mind throughout the entire process is that the *receiver's perception determines the message's meaning,* which may or may not be the meaning that the sender intended. It's commonly understood that *perception does not equal reality.* It equals our *individual reality,* and every individual has a different perception of reality.

Table 17.1   What Happens in Communication?

Sender	Interpersonal Communication	Receiver
	Message Encode . . . Decode Feedback Decode . . . Encode Misunderstanding? Perception does *not* equal reality!	

Table 17.2

What Affects Senders	What Affects Receivers
Their communication skills	Their communication skills
Their experience	Their experience
Their knowledge	Their knowledge
Their language	Their language
Their sociocultural awareness	Their sociocultural awareness
Their current attitude	Their current attitude

For example, let's say that two people standing next to each other witness the same car accident. When they are asked what they saw happen, both are very likely to have different stories, or perceptions, about what actually transpired.

Perception is determined by how we *represent* (literally *re*-present, in our own minds) what we have seen, heard, or experienced. It is created by everything we see (body language and all visual input), everything we hear (words, tonality, and all surrounding sounds), and everything we feel (all tactile sensation and surrounding emotion). It is affected by *all* the information that comes to us through our five senses, which we filter in three distinct ways.

1. **Deletion:** Everyone sees, hears, and experiences things differently. Different things are important to different people. *What isn't important to someone will be deleted.*

2. **Distortion:** Everyone distorts what he or she sees, hears, and experiences, in some way, and gives different emphasis to different things. *Individual emphasis creates distortion.*

3. **Generalization:** Everyone generalizes, draws conclusions, and decides what the things seen, heard, or experienced mean to him or her. Different things mean something different to different people. *Individual generalization creates different conclusions.*

Therefore, how someone *deletes, distorts, and generalizes* will determine how that person represents or perceives what has been communicated to him or her.

Two people can also hear the exact same thing being communicated and perceive it entirely differently. A perfect example is the analogy of "making a mountain out of a molehill." Something that is the size of a molehill—or very small and unimportant in one person's mind—might be perceived by someone else as a mountain, or a large and important matter.

Effective communication is challenging even in the best of circumstances. Communication framing will organize the process and help ensure that what everyone involved has said is understood in the way that it was intended. This will go a long way in creating more productive cross-communication—in both our business and social interactions.

KEY FOUR

Strategies for Relationships

Cultural Beliefs, Values, and Rules

The chapters in Key Four will cover the beliefs, values, and rules of the cultures you may visit and with which you may work or socialize. These clearly influence different cultures' business and social relationship strategies. If you are in management, marketing, or sales, it is essential to be able to appeal to what a culture or individual considers valuable.

Most cultures have their own unique business and social strategies. Some are more relationship-oriented, whereas others focus more intensely on outcomes. Some cultures prefer a direct approach, whereas others opt for an indirect approach. Some are willing to share personal information, whereas members of others like to keep personal information private. To build teams that work well together in the workplace or as a virtual global team, business professionals need to be aware of the various business and social strategies.

A culture's communication context has a strong impact on how various cultures perceive their own reality. Some are high context and regard everything that takes place during the communication process.

Other cultures are lower context, focusing more on what people are actually *saying*. Understanding cultural context is a great "shortcut" to successful communication.

This section will help you learn the successful relationship strategies that will enable you to *say* anything, to anyone, anywhere!

Context, Perception, and Reality

The Cross-Cultural "Shortcut"

Given all the information available on cultural relationship strategies, beliefs, values, and rules about what to do and what not to do, it's always nice to have a few shortcuts! Fortunately, one of the best shortcuts is the ability to understand context, perception, and the reality it creates. It allows us to be "people readers" without having to become cross-cultural communication experts. People readers can intelligently intuit the words beneath the words—or the words *not* being said. They can sense the *underlying meaning* of what someone is saying by considering the entire communication context. We all do this naturally to a certain extent; however, we usually do so within the communication context with which we are most familiar. We therefore need to develop our people reading skills to use with cultures that have very different communication context than our own.

Context in communication provides color, description, individual expression, and emphasis to the communication style. It helps create the desired perception in the communication process. And this perception of what someone has communicated provides his or her message with meaning, which then creates our individual realities.

Communication can have more or less context depending on the topic, the individual, and the culture. *The more context to a communication exchange, the more information there is to observe and listen to.* A communication with a lot of context will have descriptive words, expressive tonality, and demonstrative body language. This is called high-context communication. Fewer descriptive words with less tonal modulation and more subdued body language provides less context and is appropriately called low-context communication.

Although certain cultures definitely exhibit a *preference* for a higher or lower context style, this often changes with individual experience. Communication context is something you can observe and to which you can adapt without being as culturally astute. Individual preferences develop as cultures blend their communication styles through cultural overlay and homogenization. If you can determine whether someone seems to prefer a higher or lower context style, you can usually adapt and communicate effectively—regardless of that person's culture.

As noted before, high-context communicators provide information with descriptive words and use many adjectives and adverbs, which they sometimes repeat for emphasis. This adds a tone of subjectivity to the conversation, which is apparent even in business discussions. It has, at times, been referred to as fluff in the conversation. If a high-context communicator is describing a hotel, it might sound something like this: "It was a very, very nice hotel, with a really beautiful lobby that had super stylish and modern furniture. The rooms were enormous with large flat-screen TVs, and the view of the ocean was absolutely fantastic!" That definitely creates a certain perception and reality, and one that is unique to each one of us.

Higher-context individuals' tonality has lots of expression to match the words. Their vocal pitch often goes to the maximums of high and low on a tonal graph. They can make use of their entire voice range, reaching all octaves, like playing notes on a piano. They use demonstrative facial expressions and body language to emphasize what they're saying. Their hands and arms speak in unison with their words and voice. Sometimes, it looks as though high-context communicators are almost acting out what they are saying. Their style of communication has flair and conveys emotion. You nearly always know how they *feel* about the topic of discussion.

Because high-context communicators provide a great deal of information via their words, tone of voice, and body language, it's necessary to regard the *entire* communication process by listening, watching, and understanding. The words alone don't give the entire story. For example, if these individuals *say* they can do something—but their tonality, facial expression, and body language show uncertainty—you can probably conclude that they aren't sure they can do it. You can usually believe the tonality and body language more than the actual words when in doubt with high-context communicators.

If you are a manager of a high-context person, be sure to use expressive tonality and demonstrative body language when you compliment him or her on a job well done. If you don't, the employee may not believe that you really mean it. In fact, if there isn't sufficient tonality and body language, the person may even think that he or she didn't do such a great job. To be believable, credible, and congruent, you need to communicate with the appropriate context for that particular person.

I once coached an Italian executive who was sure his boss wasn't pleased with him at all. His boss would tell him that he did a "very good job" in an unexpressive tone of voice, with no emphasis or demonstrative body language. The message he conveyed to my client was that he really wasn't very happy with him; otherwise, my client assumed, he would say, "You did a *very* good job!," as though he *meant* it. In fact, my client wondered if his boss was being *sarcastic* and possibly saying the opposite of what he really wanted to say. His perception—and consequently, his reality—was hearing that he actually had *not* done a very good job. Without the kind of context he expected, my client *misread* the real meaning of the communication, which created the wrong perception and reality.

Higher-context people are usually fairly easy to *read*, because their tonality and body language give a lot of information in addition to their words. The Italian and many romantic language cultures are good examples of this. Their tone of voice and gestures often express their emotions, letting you know exactly how they feel about something.

Following are some of the major attributes of high-context communicators.

High-Context Communicators

- Speak with descriptive words and data. The *entire context* of the communication, words, tonality, and body language is regarded at all times.

- Are sensitive to emotion; therefore, it's best to approach delicate subjects indirectly rather than directly.
- Engage in more rapport building, small talk, or chitchat in the conversation.
- May discuss or *touch on* several topics at the same time.
- Often enthusiastically interrupt the conversation.
- Use many descriptive adjectives and adverbs to develop the *picture*.
- Use a very expressive tone of voice that brings life to the words.
- Exhibit animated facial expressions that correspond with words and tonality.
- Display demonstrative body language featuring many supporting hand and arm gestures.
- Tend to feel that the words' meanings are not effectively communicated if there is too little tonality and body language, which creates miscommunication and misunderstanding.
- Can be objective but often make the context of subjectivity apparent in the conversation.
- Are usually more formal, elaborate, and eloquent with their written communication until the relationship is well established.
- Are fairly easy to *read*, because their tonality and body language expresses their emotion and how they feel.

Although there is considerable *individual variation* in the use of higher- or lower-context communication within specific cultures, some cultures have a *natural tendency* to be higher-context communicators. They are the ones that you will hear elaborately describe the details of something, with lots of colorful adjectives and adverbs, accompanied by expressive tonality and body language. Some of these cultures are noted here.

Higher-Context Cultures

- The Central and South American cultures
- The southern European cultures
- The French cultures, including French-speaking Canada
- The Greek culture

- The Middle Eastern and northern/sub-Saharan African cultures
- Many tropical island cultures

In contrast, lower-context communicators focus on the meaning of the words being used to communicate. They strongly believe that too many adjectives, adverbs, or fluff hinders the conversation's real purpose. They tend to be more objective than subjective, especially in business conversations. If a low-context communicator is describing a hotel, it might sound more like this: "It was a nice hotel, with an attractive lobby. The rooms were large and had a good view of the ocean."

They use a more moderate tone of voice that exhibits less modulation. People often refer to low-context communication as more dry, with fewer tonal highs and lows on a tonal graph. Their facial expressions and body language demonstrate what they're saying; however, they're more subdued. They move their hands and arms as they speak, but much less so than high-context communicators. It is usually more difficult to determine exactly how they *feel* about the topic of discussion.

You'll likely observe that a low-context communicator gives information or context primarily through the expression of words being spoken. Data and details will accompany the communication flow to create the necessary context. It's necessary to listen carefully to precisely what the person is saying, because his or her tonality and body language provide much less context. For this reason, it is important to ask reflective questions to verify your understanding. If you are unclear about something, you can rephrase what was said in another way to confirm your comprehension of it. For example, let's say that you were confused about how someone wanted to proceed. You could *reflect back* your understanding by saying, "If I understood you correctly, you think it would be better if we got input from the entire department before we proceeded, correct?"

If you happen to be a manager of a low-context person, be sure that you don't use overly expressive tonality or excessively demonstrative body language when you compliment him or her on a job well done. Doing so might actually *embarrass* the person; in fact, the worker may even think that you are joking if you go too "over the top." Again, to be believable, credible, and congruent, you need to communicate by using the appropriate context for that particular person.

Lower-context people are usually more difficult to *read*, because they give less information and emotion through their tonality and body language. The Japanese culture is a good example of this. They are known to be some of the best negotiators, because they don't convey a lot of emotion via their tone of voice or gestures—like some of the higher-context cultures that might "give themselves away." Consequently, higher-context cultures may make concessions earlier than they otherwise would have.

Of course, even lower-context communicators can be higher context when they want to be. The Japanese are clearly higher context while singing at a karaoke bar, and the Germans are definitely higher context when saying, "Prost!" as they clang their mugs at a beer garden! But when it comes to business, they have less expressive tonality and body language, making them more difficult to read, so you aren't always sure how they feel about something.

Following are some of the major attributes of low-context communicators.

Low-Context Communicators

- Communicate primarily through words and data. As such, they listen carefully to others' words and pay less attention to tonality and body language.

- Are direct and to the point and typically don't beat around the bush when approaching a topic.

- Usually engage in less rapport building, small talk, or chitchat.

- Have more focused communication and don't stray far from the topic being discussed.

- Are less tolerant of spontaneous interruptions in the conversation.

- Use fewer descriptive adjectives and adverbs and rely more on data and details.

- Limit tonal modulations to the expressiveness needed to make a point.

- Display less animated and more subtle facial expressions.

- Use less demonstrative body language with fewer hand and arm gestures.

- Find too much tonality and body language to be distracting and even annoying. They believe that it gets in the way of what is being communicated.

- Prefer the context of what is conveyed to be more objective than subjective, especially in business conversations.

- Like to provide and receive detailed, clear, concise, and to-the-point written communication
- Are often more difficult to *read*, because they give less information and emotion via their tone of voice and gestures.

Although there is considerable *individual variation* in the use of higher- or lower-context communication within specific cultures, some cultures have a *natural tendency* to be lower-context communicators. They are the ones that will communicate their message clearly and directly, without elaborate descriptions and overly expressive tonality and body language. Some of these cultures are listed here.

Lower-Context Cultures

- The Germanic, Scandinavian, and Nordic cultures
- The Swiss German culture
- The Dutch and German-speaking Belgian cultures
- The northern European cultures
- The British culture
- The Japanese culture

There are many variables that create higher- or lower-context communication styles, including mother tongue languages, environment, personal experience, and individual preference. As a result, many cultures are in the *middle* of the spectrum and can move rather easily between high- and low-context communication.

The important thing to keep in mind about communication context, perception, and reality is that we are *all* people readers. If the other person has perceived what you communicated "out of context" from what you expected, it's because that person *misread* it in some way. This can lead to miscommunication, misunderstanding, and conflict, especially when different cultures are involved in the interaction. When this happens, it's helpful to ask yourself the following three questions:

1. Was the cause of the miscommunication or misunderstanding *verbal* or *nonverbal*?
2. Was my communication *overly expressive* with *too much* information?
3. Was my communication *not expressive enough* with *too little* information?

These three questions will help you quickly identify where the communication breakdown may have occurred. And once you know where the *breakdown* was, you can reposition yourself to *break through* any remaining communication barriers.

When it comes to multicultural relationship strategies, an understanding of high- and low-context communication styles will help you adapt without having to know a lot about a particular culture. It's a shortcut that gives you the ability to be a spontaneous *people reader*, which will enable you to communicate more successfully with anyone, anywhere!

chapter 19

Business and Social Behavioral Styles

Where Do You Start?

To understand and effectively utilize relationship strategies, it is essential to educate oneself on various cultures' workplace and social behavior styles. Today's global business marketplace features a multinational workforce in nearly every country—and in nearly every industry. It can be challenging to be able to work together successfully, especially when the expected behavioral protocol varies from culture to culture *and* from industry to industry.

This is clearly an obstacle for business travelers and expatriates. It's not always easy to adapt to the behavior styles of a country or culture that might be very different from your own. Circles Of Excellence has had some interesting experiences doing just that in Geneva, Switzerland. In the words of one of my business colleagues, we couldn't just pull out our blue U.S. passports and say, "We'll do it our way!"

Every country and culture has preferred business etiquette and different approaches and expectations regarding both business and social behavior. These behavior styles are developed over the years and are part of an individual's cultural layers.

One of the major differences in behavior styles is how different cultures view relationship development and business objectives. Some cultures tend to be more *relationship-oriented*, whereas others are more objective- or *outcome-oriented*.

It's necessary to spend more time with relationship-oriented cultures developing a personal connection before pursuing a business goal, objective, or outcome. It's necessary to engage in this kind of social behavior to form business rapport and trust. For example, many of the Asian cultures are very relationship-oriented. It takes considerable time to build genuine, trustworthy, and interdependent connections in Korea, China, and Japan. As far as these cultures are concerned, relationships are the most important element of business. They nearly always consider the impact that something will have on a relationship before they pursue a business objective. If there is a chance that they might damage an important relationship in the process, they will likely find an alternative way to accomplish their objective. Consequently, they may take a more *indirect* approach to business communication and outcome achievement. The result is important to them, of course; however, if it comes at the expense of the relationship, they are likely to consider the relationship first. They believe that "if you take care of the relationship, it will take care of you."

Outcome-oriented cultures are more objective-driven. They develop business relationships more quickly and consequently spend less time developing rapport and trust. They usually don't require as much small talk before discussing business. The Swedish, Swiss German, and German cultures tend to lean this way in their business exchanges. Relationships are important to them; however, they require less social interaction and small talk for business communication and form relationships that are more independent than interdependent.

These cultures take a more *direct* business approach and quickly get to the point about what they want to accomplish. The purpose of their communication is to achieve the business goal, objective, or outcome. They feel that because this objective is the reason for forming the relationship in the first place, the objective should be the primary focus. They believe that "you can please many people some of the time, but it's not possible to please *everyone* all the time."

Figure 19.1 shows how various cultures relate with respect to outcome- and relationship-oriented behavior styles.

Of course, an individual's *profession* also affects cultural behavior styles—and business professions also have cultural distinctions. Just

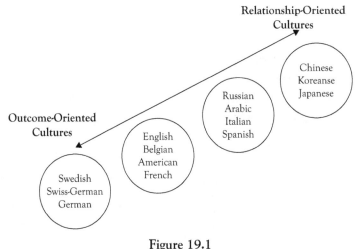

Figure 19.1
Cultural Relationship and Outcome Orientation

like a country's culture, they have varying approaches and expectations regarding business and social behavior. For example, human resources personnel are usually very *relationship-oriented* in their behavior. After all, they interact with people every day and are quite aware of how their behavior affects relationships. They are therefore likely to focus on the interactions among people, both socially and in business.

On the other hand, those working in the accounting department are very different from human resources staff. Accountants interact with people less frequently and focus primarily on facts, figures, and numbers (that is, the objective or outcome). As a result, they are more *outcome-oriented* in business. Even when its purpose is to accomplish a business objective, social interaction can often be more challenging for them.

A few years ago, we helped accountants at a large firm build better relationships with their clients. The accountants had what is commonly known in the business world as the banker's mentality: Their primary focus was numbers, which can make for a rather dry conversation. Because of the slow economy at that time, the accountants had been asked to wine and dine their clients to actively develop business. This was not something they were accustomed to doing! For the most part, they worked on their own, behind a desk, for hours at a time. To many of them, conversation consisted of whether something was in the

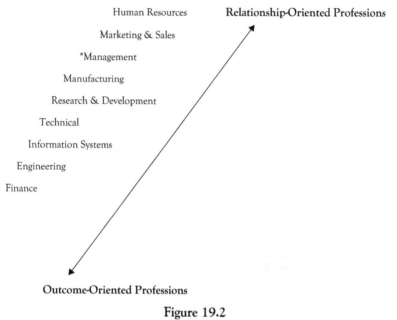

Figure 19.2
Professional Relationship and Outcome Orientation

red or the black. Socially entertaining their clients was a daunting prospect for them. They were therefore forced to step out of their comfort zone—their outcome-driven accountants' shoes—and learn to become more relationship-oriented. Clearly, this wasn't necessarily an easy or comfortable thing for them to do.

Figure 19.2 shows how various professions relate with respect to outcome- and relationship-oriented behavior styles.

Note where "*Management" is positioned on the graph in Figure 19.2—near the top of the scale toward relationship-oriented professions. This implies management for *any* of the listed professions. All too often, people in the outcome-oriented professions are promoted to the management level because of their ability, *without* the necessary relationship orientation to manage effectively. This type of promotion is one of the biggest challenges in business today, because managers from *every profession* need to be more relationship-oriented.

It is therefore essential that these managers receive the necessary leadership and communication skills training to be successful. Without it, they are likely to become frustrated and wonder whether they're "cut out" for management. We've heard many a frustrated boss proclaim, "I didn't ask for all these people problems. If this is what management is all about, I don't need it!"

Management styles and expectations also vary in different cultures. Although styles change and evolve, the following guidelines are helpful if you work with managers in these cultures or if you manage people from these cultures.

Management Styles of English-Speaking Cultures

- Use democratic management style
- Engage in participative decision making
- Are motivated by earnings and recognition
- Have an I or me orientation
- Take personal initiative
- Prefer individual autonomy

Management Styles of Central and South American Cultures

- Use an autocratic management style
- Engage in top-down decision making
- Are motivated by earnings and recognition
- Have a we or us orientation
- Take team initiative
- Prefer the security of group affiliation

Management Styles of Southern European Cultures

- Use an autocratic management style
- Engage in top-down decision making
- Are motivated by quality of life
- Have a we or us orientation
- Take team initiative
- Prefer the security of group affiliation

Management Styles of Northern European Cultures

- Use a democratic management style
- Engage in participative decision making
- Are motivated by quality of life
- Have a we or us orientation
- Admire personal and team initiative
- Prefer a humanistic approach

Management Styles of Asian Pacific Cultures

- Use an autocratic management style
- Engage in top-approved, group-oriented decision making
- Are motivated by earnings and recognition for the group or organization
- Have a we or us orientation
- Take team initiative
- Achieve self-identify through group affiliation

Another cultural behavior style difference is how people feel about sharing personal or private information, something that's usually determined by what a particular individual considers *appropriate* personal or private information to share in a social or business setting. And as it does vary from one person to another, the definition of *appropriate* clearly varies from culture to culture as well. Sharing these kinds of things is one of the behavioral styles that can create real discomfort for more *private-oriented* cultures.

Privacy is important to everyone, and it's becoming even more important in this day and age. We hear about the problems with the privacy issues of social media nearly every day—one reason many people are hesitant to become involved in social media. Many private-oriented cultures don't want their personal details, photos, and videos being shared in the first place. The thought of these private things being improperly exposed is incomprehensible. Even for business enterprises, social media, privacy, and security have become a top priority.

More private cultures are quite protective of what personal information they allow to become public. They generally define this kind of information as anything that they don't consider necessary to share to further a social or business relationship.

These cultures share what they consider *appropriate* personal information socially; however, they may not be comfortable sharing the same information in a business scenario. To them, personal information is not business related, and for that reason, it isn't necessary to share. The phrase *too much information*—or *TMI* for short—is now commonly used when someone says more than needs to be said.

Social relationships should include more sharing of personal information than a business relationship does for these private cultures. This is partially because social relationships build friendships, which *require* that the parties know some personal information about one another. However, these individuals reserve true "friendship" for a close social relationship—one that they take considerable time to develop. If a social relationship isn't particularly close, you are acquaintances—not friends—and someone with whom they will share less personal information.

There is a distinct separation between social and business relationships in these cultures. "Business is business" as far as they're concerned, and knowing the details of someone's personal or private life *isn't required*. Building rapport is a business exchange about their position, job, or company. In the workplace, these cultures are likely to call coworkers colleagues or peers rather than friends. Members of these cultures feel out of their *comfort zone* when someone asks them questions about their family, social life, health, or other personal subjects.

You can usually expect that people from these cultures will ask fewer personal questions when marketing or selling to them. Consequently, it's best to avoid asking personal questions yourself until the relationship is well established or until the other person initiates a personal question. If the other person volunteers this kind of private information or asks you a question of a similar nature, you can safely assume you won't offend him or her if you ask similar questions in return.

It is usually more challenging when managing someone from a private-oriented culture to get them to open up and discuss personal issues. For example, it won't be easy for them to discuss if personal problems at home are affecting their job performance. It is helpful for managers to be empathetic and *ask only what is absolutely necessary* so that these individuals don't feel like they are being exposed.

Keep in mind that there is also a *range* of how private someone is *within private-oriented cultures*. Individual perceptions could be very different based on what they perceive as private or personal. Case in point: Younger people are clearly becoming more open and less private due to the ease of social media and text communication. Our individual personalities, preferences, and our family and friends' influence are all factors that affect how we view privacy. In addition, cultural blending and homogenization are changing what cultures feel is appropriate personal information to share—or not share. With that caveat, the following are some of the cultures that tend to be more private-oriented.

Private-Oriented Cultures

- The Swiss culture
- The Germanic, Scandinavian, and Nordic cultures
- Some northern European cultures
- The British culture

In contrast, many other cultures are *public-oriented* with their personal lives. They are quite comfortable sharing personal or private information, even at times with someone they have just met. They are happy to discuss their family, social life, health, and other personal subjects in both social and business relationships. Some cultures are even comfortable discussing their personal finances and will ask you questions about yours as well. For them, this is simply a natural part of relationship development.

People usually initiate personal questions in new relationships as a means of getting to know another person. Members of public-oriented cultures simply consider this to be part of the process of building social and business relationships—and they expect the same from those with whom they interact. They feel it's a necessary element of developing rapport and trust, and they seek a reciprocal exchange of personal information to further the business relationship.

When marketing or selling to these cultures, you can usually expect that they will ask more personal questions. You'll also find that answering their questions openly will develop the relationship much more quickly. These individuals naturally volunteer personal information in their business relationships and are perfectly comfortable having their social and business lives overlap.

You'll notice that it is easier to get people from public-oriented cultures to open up and discuss personal issues when managing them. They

Private-Oriented: Public and private lives are minimally integrated. Personal information is separated by what is considered "appropriate" to share for business. Sharing too much personal information in business relationships is unnatural and uncomfortable.

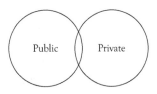

Public-Oriented: Public and private lives are more integrated. Private information is an integral part of the relationship development in business to develop rapport and trust. Sharing personal information in business relationships is natural, comfortable, and expected.

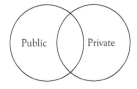

Figure 19.3

Public and Private Business Comfort Zones

are comfortable having a conversation about things that may be affecting their job performance—*as long as they aren't being put on the defensive.* The questions you're asking should never be personal to the extent that they are perceived as intrusive.

And, of course, there is a *range* within these cultures as to how public-oriented someone actually is. People's personalities, preferences, and influence of family and friends affect what they feel is appropriate to share. With that caveat, the following are some of the cultures that tend to be more public-oriented.

Public-Oriented Cultures

- The Central and South American cultures
- Some southern European cultures
- Some Asian Pacific cultures
- Parts of the U.S. culture, especially the Southern U.S.

Most other cultures are in the middle range and will comfortably share moderate amounts of personal or private information. They may have a more conservative view of what is appropriate to share than the public-oriented cultures, but they aren't as reserved about what they share than the private-oriented cultures.

Understanding the expected protocol for the social and business behavior styles of different cultures can greatly enhance the likelihood of successful sales, marketing, and management in today's global workplace. It's wise to plan relationship strategies in advance of any new multicultural business connection.

chapter 20

Understanding Cultural Beliefs, Values, and Rules

The Roots of Every Culture

Cultural beliefs, values, and rules are *intricately woven into the very fabric of a culture*. They strengthen, reinforce, give structure, maintain order, and ultimately become the standards and norms that give a culture its unique identity. In the same way that a tree's roots ground and nourish a seedling to give it strength throughout its life, the roots of our native culture ground and nourish us from childhood to adulthood.

A variety of elements, from environment to mother tongue languages, influence what cultures believe and value. On an individual basis, our culture is the foundation that guides our beliefs, values, behavior, and how we view life. These beliefs and values influence the way we all experience important aspects of our lives.

Beliefs are defined by BusinessDictionary.com as follows:

Assumptions and convictions that are held to be true, by an individual or a group, regarding concepts, events, people, and things

Individual and group beliefs are the *collective ideas* that create a culture's values, which then determine what is most important to the individual or group. They are further reinforced, and often enforced, by the creation of cultural rules. This inner weaving of our cultural beliefs, values, and rules gives distinction to the color, texture, and pattern of the cultural fabric and become what is known as the cultural standards or norms.

Some cultural values are passed down from one generation to the next. New values are created as necessary to keep up with environmental and cultural changes, and they often lead to the creation of new rules of conduct and behavior. These new rules then generate standards or norms to give structure and stability to the culture.

Cultural values are defined by BusinessDictionary.com as follows:

> *The commonly held standards of what is acceptable or unacceptable, important or unimportant, right or wrong, workable or unworkable, etc., in a community or society.*

According to sociologists, culture is the totality of socially transmitted behavior patterns, arts, beliefs, institutions, and all other products of human work and thought. These patterns, traits, and products are considered the expression of a particular community, period, class, or population.

Values describe the beliefs and accepted standards of an individual or culture. A set of values may be categorized into a value system. Values may be subjective or apply to groups. They vary with people and cultures. Some types of values include ethical/moral, doctrinal/ideological, political/religious, social, aesthetic, and so on.

Understanding what a particular culture believes and values is clearly important in developing successful business and social relationship strategies with that culture. Each culture has norms for the business and social protocol, expected behavior, and appropriate conduct based on their shared beliefs and values.

Enculturation is the natural and unconscious process by which we develop our native cultural instincts, beliefs, and values. We're all aware of the United States' status as a melting pot of hundreds of different ethnic groups, each of which is a distinct culture in itself. Most immigrants have an existing relationship with their native culture as well as with their newly acquired culture. The assimilation that occurs when the pure native culture is slowly lost as it merges with the new is referred to as *acculturation*. Eventually, the two cultures overlap, creating a uniquely blended cultural perspective, which becomes part of the individual's cultural layers of identity.

As immigrants experience acculturation, they adopt another set of cultural beliefs, values, and rules that initially coexist with their native cultures. After some time, these begin to replace what existed from the native culture. It is rare that immigrants remain truly bicultural and continue to use two sets of cultural norms simultaneously and equally. Their newly acquired cultural norms eventually become dominant and absorb the characteristics of the native culture's norms.

A trend known as *retro-acculturation* has also recently emerged. This is the ancestral search for the ethnic identity or roots that immigrants have lost. Many cultures, including the U.S. American culture, have third- and fourth-generation immigrants who are using technology to trace their ancestry and search for this lost identity. Some people have even lost the knowledge of what an immigrant's native language originally *was*. The Afro-American culture is an example of one where this language loss has frequently occurred.

When it comes to cultural beliefs, values, and rules, *different is normal*; that is, what is considered normal is relative to the culture. Every culture creates a level of conformity that allows people to become integrated and socialized into the culture in which they live. Cultural values are a culture's ideas about what is good, fair, right, just, and appropriate—ideas can vary vastly from one culture to another.

For example, *individualism* is a commonly held core value in the U.S. American culture. Members of this culture look favorably upon the freedom to accomplish goals individually and do things in a way uniquely their own. It indeed provides the foundation for entrepreneurship and the ability to create enterprises based on individual interests and expertise. The United States is a country that proudly states, "Anything is possible, and whether you believe you can or can't, you're right!" The value of individuality extends to everything one does—including behavior, appearance, and choice of fashion or attire.

In contrast, one of the important Japanese core values is *conformity*, a quality that the Japanese believe creates a feeling of unity within the country, group, community, or company. Engaging in behavior that is outside the norm could be perceived as offensive by the Japanese culture. It is inappropriate to wear anything that makes you stand out or something that might be considered unique or flashy. The Japanese saying "The nail that sticks up gets hit with the hammer" describes how strongly they feel about the value of conformity.

Cultures frequently seem to have conflicting value systems. Cultural values are shared or *collective*, and they can apply to the culture as a whole or to specific groups within it. When values differ between a culture's groups, it affects the shared values that all members have in common. And when these distinct group values clash with the shared values, a value conflict is likely to occur.

For example, some would say that one of the important values in the United States is the freedom to achieve success, wealth, and power. However, some groups within the United States would argue that not everyone has an equal opportunity to achieve these things, thereby creating a value conflict. The actual shared value in common might be that the United States shares the "American work ethic," which encourages hard work to achieve as much success, wealth, and power as possible.

Contradictions and value conflicts also exist due to inconsistencies between what people say they believe and what they actually *do*. This requires that we distinguish between members of culture's beliefs and actions. The *ideal culture* refers to the values that the culture professes to believe, whereas the *actual culture* refers to the values that it acts upon in reality. Despite the contradictions, cultural values still maintain order and influence behavior.

Many organizations have recently created business behavior values to reflect the company's *ideals*. Some take it a step further and have individual departments adopt these values and then further define them to reflect the *ideals* of their department. Businesses clearly function more effectively with company values in place. It's something we encourage all companies that we consult with to develop if they don't currently have them.

Social behavior values emerge as cultures and groups change with the times. These reflect the *ideals* of the current society or groups within the society. They set the social rules and norms for interpersonal conduct and influence the etiquette, trends, fashion, and attire, among other things.

Cultural groups can greatly affect the social values and resulting norms of the cultural whole. Groups make decisions based on what they believe the predominant group values and rules *should* be. This is apparent when we consider the various political parties, educational institutions, organizations, associations, clubs, and so on, that exist within almost all societies.

Members of a culture typically make group decisions by using one or a combination of three processes that include decisions by *majority* (more than half the total agree on a decision), *seniority* (the most senior leaders decide), or *consensus* (an agreement or decision reached by the group as a whole). Business, political, and social decision making will vary in their use of these three processes from culture to culture.

For example, decision making in the United States is characteristically democratic, meaning that decisions are frequently made by the majority. In many Latin American cultures, decisions are often made and enforced by senior leaders. Asian cultures habitually make decisions using both consensus and seniority. It's essential for business professionals to know how decisions are likely to be made in the cultures with whom they're working.

For some cultures, religious beliefs have become values that clearly affect group behavior. Religious rules regarding appearance, attire, and prayer often coexist in the work environment—and when religious beliefs overlap into the business world, it can be a challenging situation to manage. We recently worked with a U.S.-based construction firm where emotions ran high over building a mosque in a predominately Christian neighborhood. This required great diplomacy on management's part as they addressed and resolved the various concerns.

The place of women in society and business is also governed by cultural beliefs, values, and rules. Even a seemingly mundane action such as a handshake between women and men can incite questions in some cultures. We need to ask: "Are handshakes between men and women allowed in this culture? If so, who should extend their hand first?" and "What are the rules and protocol between men and women?" Asking these questions in advance can help avoid embarrassment and potential cultural offense.

For example, many Muslim cultures prohibit men from shaking the hand of a woman to whom he is not related. There was a good example of this at the 2012 Summer Olympics in England, when an Iranian Paralympic silver medal winner refused to shake hands with Kate Middleton (Mountbatten-Windsor), Duchess of Cambridge. Business professionals must be aware of the appropriate conduct between men and women in various cultures.

Governing parties and rulers clearly have a powerful influence on a culture's current beliefs, norms, values, and rules. New leadership in countries that undergo revolutions can completely transform the previously existing norms and rules—or at least this seems to be the case from an outsider's perspective. In reality, a culture's underlying core beliefs and values can often take generations to change.

This is especially true if family and friends privately hold onto and reinforce these traditional beliefs and values. This was the case with many people in East Germany and the Eastern European countries while under communist control. On the surface, they seemed to be functioning completely and wholly as communist countries. However, the underlying beliefs and values associated with freedom remained as a hope for a better future, and elder generations passed these beliefs and values down to the younger generations. I've had the opportunity to work with many people from Eastern Europe who have shared with me how important it was to keep this hope alive.

Understanding what a particular culture, country, or individual values most is essential for developing successful business marketing strategies. For example, you want to emphasize how a given product's or service's characteristics and qualities are congruent with what a consumer values. Doing so will create a meaningful perception and position the product in a positive, appealing way. Anyone who is in the business of marketing or advertising is aware of this.

Business professionals need to make their products, services, ideas, material, and messages meaningful and *valuable* to the culture, country, or individual with whom they are working. Sales professionals need to frame their marketing messages and material to target and reflect the dominant values and current trends. This will put a positive spin on how the people to whom they are presenting perceive their products, services, and ideas.

Let's say that you are selling a car in France. You might emphasize maneuverability, as well as the car's design and aesthetics—all of which appeal to the French culture and its values.

However, you'd want to highlight different features if you are selling a car in Japan. In that case, you might emphasize the advanced technology, the compact size, and how it addresses Japanese buyers' needs—all elements that appeal to that particular culture and its values. And if you are selling a car in the United States, you might emphasize luxury, individuality, and spaciousness—all desirable benefits to members of the U.S. culture.

The following are examples of some values that you would want to reflect in business messages, material, and marketing or advertising campaigns for Europe, Japan, and the United States. Although these are general tendencies that vary among individuals within the cultures, they still have a strong influence on what is valued as important.

European Values

- Aesthetics
- Intellectualism
- Tradition
- Leisure
- Enjoyment
- Social appeal
- Family
- Friends

Japanese Values

- Collectivism
- Group benefit
- Conformity
- Harmony
- Determination
- Advancement
- Self-improvement
- Humility

U.S. American Values

- Freedom
- Equality
- Individuality
- Entrepreneurship

- Competition
- Success
- Power
- Mobility

Cultural rules are developed for the purpose of reinforcing a culture's values. These rules govern societal behavior and dictate what a culture believes to be good, right, and just. They can be enforced *formally* through laws and legislation or *informally* through reprimands and warnings. But even a culture's informal rules will serve to promote considerable societal control.

Cultural rules are described according to sociologists as the following:

Each culture dictates rules for certain, expected behavior based on shared values and beliefs.

Formal rules are written down, and breaking them generally results in some form of punishment. Cultural societies have large numbers of these rules; examples are traffic, crime, and public safety laws.

Informal rules aren't necessarily written down; rather, they are basically guidelines that people follow in their daily lives. If people don't follow them, they usually aren't formally punished. However, there may be a reprimand, warning, or a display of disapproving nonverbal communication. Whether these rules are officially written or not, you'll know when you're breaking one.

I experienced this kind of disapproving nonverbal communication firsthand when I moved to Dallas. There was an informal rule among fashion-conscious women not to wear white shoes between Labor Day and Easter. My faux pas was a result of my belief that if the weather was hot, white sandals were appropriate—even in the winter. As fashion in Dallas has evolved, I've seen this rule now stretch to allow white shoes to be worn after the first day of spring up until the last day of summer. And with prolonged warmer weather this is now extending into fall, so possibly at some point in the future, this rule will cease to exist altogether! Although this is a minor infraction, there are clearly times where breaking an informal rule can potentially create problems or ruin a business deal. When we do public training seminars in parts of Europe, it is expected that we will provide lunch, including wine, at our cost.

It is also likely that lunch will be an hour and a half rather than an hour. If we were to send attendees to dine on their own, at their own cost, it could be thought of as impolite. I actually rather like that rule and certainly do prefer their idea of a more leisurely lunch!

Understanding cultural beliefs, values, and rules is one of the most important things we can do to further our professional and social relationships. It is essential for everyone to learn the common norms of the countries and cultures with which they work or travel to.

CHAPTER
21

The Cross-Cultural Potter's Wheel

Don't Create a Warped Relationship!

Cross-cultural relationships are much like clay on a potter's wheel. In the same way that a potter molds and creates pieces with great care, cross-cultural relationships need to be molded and creates with great care on the global communication stage. And the more time and care that one puts into such a creation, the more useful and beautiful it will be. To be successful, you need to consider the clay's type, consistency, and malleability. You need to know the best shape, design, color, and glaze for the pot you want to create.

The same applies to cross-cultural relationships. The more time and care that is put into developing the relationship, the more productive and enjoyable it will be. To be successful, you need to consider the individual's culture, characteristics, and what communication approach you should use to work most effectively with him or her. You need to know the most appropriate words, tonality, body language, and rapport style that will best suit the relationship you want to create.

Anyone who's ever thrown a clay pot on a potter's wheel knows that the most important part of the process is to get the clay *centered* on the wheel. And if *you* aren't centered before you throw, you won't hit the target. The clay will land *off-center*, thereby creating a wobble in the wheel. If this happens, you will create a warped pot—no matter how hard you try to make it symmetrical. If the clay lands completely off-center, bits of it may start flying off in all directions!

The same applies to cross-cultural relationships. If *you* aren't centered before you speak, you might say the wrong words in the wrong way and fail to hit the target you're aiming for. You'll say something off-center, and others won't perceive you as you intended. That creates a "wobble" in the relationship. And if this happens, no matter how hard you try to recover and reframe what was said, you may create a warped relationship. Indeed, if what you say is completely off-center, you may unintentionally offend someone—and cause their response to fly off in all directions!

This analogy takes us full circle back to the first key of this book, which you may recall was titled "Create Proactive Cross-Cultural Communication." To be proactive and center the clay on the potter's wheel, you must know something about pottery craftsmanship. You have to watch the spin of the wheel and be able to judge its speed and velocity. You need to adjust your stance and aim to match your throw as the wheel spins. Finally, you throw the lump of clay onto the wheel. If everything works successfully in unison, you hit the target *on center*—and there is no need to redo anything. You can begin molding and designing your pot, and it will be perfectly symmetrical.

To be proactive and center yourself when communicating interpersonally, you must know something about the individual with whom you are speaking and his or her culture. You also need to observe the person's style (fast or slow communication, high or low context, etc.) to see if he or she truly does display the cultural tendencies you expected. If necessary, you need to adjust your words, tonality, and body language to match the other person's style. You want to frame your communication in the best possible way for the individual and culture. Finally, you say what you need to say. Remember, what you *say* is conveyed through your *words*, *tonality*, and *body language*. If what you say is well received, you have hit the target on center and you won't need to be reactive or to reframe anything. You can proceed with the communication exchange, and nothing will be off-center or out of balance.

Proactive cross-cultural communication becomes easier to accomplish as you practice and gain experience. As you communicate with different cultures, their styles and approaches become part of your individual cultural layers—a cultural overlay that then becomes integrated into the very essence of your being. You begin to naturally and easily create rapport and trust with different cultures, and you will be able to adapt and go beyond any preexisting cultural perceptions. You find yourself connecting on the *human cultural level*, which is at the heart of what every culture has in common. But whatever you do—proactive awareness is the first step!

The following description of Maslow's four steps to learning will help guide you through the process of successful cross-cultural communication.

Maslow's Four Steps When Communicating Cross-Culturally

1. **Unconscious incompetence:** You don't know that you don't know.

   In this step, ignorance is bliss. You are not yet aware that you need to learn something about cross-cultural communication. You think that you can say something to someone in the exact same way that you would like to have it said to you. And as we have learned, this is clearly not the case!

2. **Conscious incompetence:** You know that you need to know.

   This is the step where you become aware that you need to learn something about cross-cultural communication. You may have made a cultural faux pas or possibly even offended someone unintentionally.

3. **Conscious competence:** You know that you know, but you need to consciously think about what you know.

   Here, you know that you are able to successfully communicate with various cultures; however, you need to think consciously about it. It doesn't come naturally *yet*. Readers of this book are likely to be at this step.

4. **Unconscious competence:** You know that you know, and you don't need to think about it!

   When you reach this point, you know that you are able to successfully communicate with various cultures without having to think about it. Your multicultural communication comes naturally and easily, and you are fully centered in your cultural awareness.

Being centered is the key to accomplishing anything of importance that requires focus and concentration. *Business* professionals are much more productive than *busy-ness* professionals. Global business communication is here to stay, and trying to communicate successfully in cross-cultural relationships, without being centered, is like trying to drive a car with the emergency brakes on!

KEY FIVE

Success Leaves Clues

Cultural Clues, Do's, and Taboos

The chapters in Key Five will cover the cultural clues, do's, and taboos that you must keep in mind to enjoy successful business and social relationships. It highlights what works and what doesn't work with cultures around the world. Everyone in today's global business environment needs to be aware of the social and business etiquette for different cultures. It's essential to avoid those embarrassing faux pas!

You don't need to reinvent the wheel to understand what people from various cultures appreciate and don't appreciate. It's a matter of learning what *their* expectations are and then understanding how they affect *your* expectations. In business relationships, it's important to define, clarify, or avoid any acronyms, abbreviations, analogies, slang, or sports jargon. Very often, people take these *literally*, and you get a question like, "Where exactly *is* left field?"

Most important, body language gestures can sabotage a casual visitor or the most astute business professional. And all the cultural intelligence in the world won't matter if you unintentionally offend someone with your body language gestures.

Success leaves clues—and this chapter is where you will find them. However, keep in mind that *knowledge* is simply information, *wisdom* knows what to do with the information, but *action* is the power that leads to success!

Body Language Gestures to Avoid

Keep Your Fingers to Yourself!

Success leaves clues, or as you will see in some instances cited throughout the chapter, *the lack of success leave clues*. Gestures are one of the first things to come to mind when people imagine a cultural faux pas. These motions can quickly sabotage anyone, including the most savvy business professionals. People from every culture, including various country leaders and several U.S. presidents, have been guilty of unintentionally offending people from different cultures through the use of inappropriate gestures. When it comes to body language gestures, the wisest advice might be to *keep your fingers to yourself*.

This chapter highlights some of the most common hand gestures that are likely to be offensive in many cultures throughout the world.

One of the earliest and most infamous offenses for the OK hand gesture (Figure 22.1) took place in the 1950s, when President Nixon was disembarking a plane in Brazil. Standing on the plane steps, he flashed a broad smile and gestured with a double-handed OK sign. In Brazil, Germany, Russia, and many other countries around the world, the OK sign is a very offensive gesture because it is used to depict a private bodily

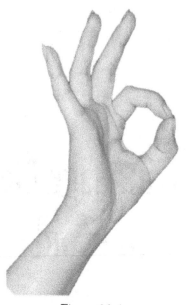

Figure 22.1
OK Hand Gesture
Graphic by Photos.com

orifice. In defense of President Nixon's ignorance, the OK sign actually *does* mean "okay" in the United States; in Japan, it means "money," and it is commonly used to signify "zero" in France. Clearly the OK sign isn't offensive *everywhere;* however, it is not OK to use in many parts of the world, nor does it necessarily mean "okay"!

Yet another president—President George H.W. Bush—made headlines in Canberra, Australia, in 1992 when he gave a *palm inward* V for victory or peace sign (Figure 22.2) while riding in his limousine. In essence, he greeted the Australians by flashing their version of the symbol for "Up yours!"—the Australian equivalent of the U.S. middle finger up. He later issued a formal apology, which was humorous, considering that it was just the day before when he stated that, "I'm a man that knows every gesture you've ever seen—and I haven't learned a new one since I've been here!"

Many people are aware that the victory gesture was made popular by Winston Churchill in England during WWII. However, it's important to take heed of where you are in the world, because if you make this signal with your *palm facing inward* in the United Kingdom, South Africa, and several other countries throughout the world, it carries the same insulting meaning that it does in Australia.

Figure 22.2
V for Victory or Peace Sign Gesture
Graphic by Photos.com

Figure 22.3
Hook 'Em Horns or Il Cornuto Gesture
Graphic by ShutterStock

More recently, on Inauguration Day 2005, President George W. Bush raised his fist, *with the index and little finger extended*, to give the time honored hook 'em horns gesture (Figure 22.3) of the Texas Longhorn football team to the marching band of his alma mater, the University of Texas. Newspapers around the world expressed their astonishment at the use of such a gesture. In Oslo, Norway, this gesture is associated with a satanic gesture to salute Satan. Italians refer to it as il cornuto, which means that you are being cuckolded (that is, that your wife is cheating on you!). And it's considered a curse in some African countries. It is clearly an offensive gesture in many parts of the world.

That being said, it's also a sign of good luck that's used in jewelry in Venezuela and Brazil, and U.S. football referees regularly use the gesture to indicate a second down. In American Sign Language, it combines the letters i, l, and y to mean "I love you." Who would have ever guessed how many different meanings a single hand gesture could have?

A similar gesture in Hawaii is made with a closed fist and the thumb and little finger extended, known as the shaka. President Obama, who lived much of his life in Hawaii, makes this gesture frequently to signal "hang loose"—or relax and take it easy. Although it is positive in nature, it's often been confused with the Texas hook 'em horns or il cornuto gesture.

So, when it comes to all the variations of the hook 'em horns gesture, it's best to use with caution.

The thumbs up signal (Figure 22.4) is commonly used in many cultures. Hitchhikers around the world, for instance, use it to try to hitch a ride, while coaches, parents, and other leaders signify a job well done. However, if it is used in Australia or the Middle East—especially if it is thrust up as a typical hitchhiking gesture would be—it means essentially "Up yours!" or "Sit on this!" And if the gesture is thrust forward in Greece, it means basically the same thing. It is also considered offensive in much of South America, West Africa, and several other countries throughout the world. In northern Spain, it is a political gesture for the Basque movement, so it may bring your motives to question if you use it there.

The thumbs up gesture can create some real problems for those who count on their fingers. In Germany and Hungary, the upright thumb is used to represent the number 1; however, it represents the number 5 in Japan. Take heed all you global negotiators: there is a big difference between 1 and 5 million!

The thumbs down gesture typically connotes a negative response or "no." It is thought that it may have originated in ancient Rome, where it meant to "plunge the sword into the victim." Whether it's thumbs up

Figure 22.4
Thumbs Up Gesture
Graphic by Photos.com

or thumbs down, it is wise not to use these gestures among cultures with which you are unfamiliar. For the most part, it may simply be wisest to *keep your thumbs to yourself!*

As a professional speaker, I am all too aware that simply *pointing with the index finger* (Figure 22.5) at something or someone can be offensive in many cultures. It is considered a very rude thing to do in China, Japan, Indonesia, Latin America, and many other countries around the world. In Europe, it's simply thought of as impolite. And in many African countries, the index finger is used only for pointing at inanimate objects, *never* at people.

If I am in a professional situation where I need to point to where something is located or to signal that someone in the audience can ask his or her question, I always use an open hand with all my fingers as close together as possible.

Curling the index finger with the palm facing up (Figure 22.6) is a common gesture the people in the United States use to beckon someone to come closer. However, it is considered a rude gesture in Slovakia, China, East Asia, Malaysia, Singapore, the Philippines, and many other parts of the world. It's considered extremely impolite to use this gesture

Figure 22.5
Finger Point Gesture
Graphic by ShutterStock

Figure 22.6
Finger Curl or Beckon Gesture
Graphic by Microsoft Clip Art

with people. It is used only to beckon dogs in many Asian countries—and using it in the Philippines can actually get you arrested!

The finger curl beckon is thought to be very seductive in Latin America and is used as a "come on" by a man to a woman. People in Australia and Indonesia use it to beckon prostitutes, whereas the gesture may be mistaken to mean "good-bye" in southern Europe. The appropriate way to beckon someone in Europe and China (among other countries) is to face the palm of your hand downward and move your fingers in a scratching motion. However,

Figure 22.7
Fig Gesture
Graphic by Photos.com

given all this gesture's various meanings, it's probably wise to avoid using it altogether!

The fig gesture is formed by making a fist with the thumb between the knuckles of the index and middle finger. It is of Roman origin and originally meant good luck and fertility. This led to its association with the sexual organs, often in an insulting manner. In much of Asia, Italy, Greece, Turkey, France, Indonesia, Japan, Russia, Serbia, and many other countries, this is considered an obscene gesture. The "fig" is taken as a threatening gesture in India. In Slovakia it means "no" or that you can't have something.

On the other hand, citizens of Portugal and Brazil believe it to be a symbol of good luck and use it as a trinket in jewelry. It is also the symbol for the letter t in American Sign Language.

Although this gesture isn't as commonly used as some of the others, it can certainly be offensive when used in the wrong places.

You form the open hand or moutza gesture by opening your palm with your fingers apart and extending your arm toward someone (Figure 22.8). This may seem harmless enough to many Westerners; most would simply assume that the other person is waving to them. However, if someone does it with a more abrupt arm extension, its meaning changes to something like, "Enough is enough," or "Let me stop you right there." In other words, "Talk to the hand, because the face isn't listening!"

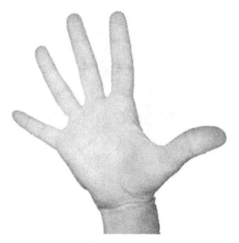

Figure 22.8
Open Hand or Moutza Gesture
Graphic by Microsoft Clip Art

In Greece—where the term *moutza* originated—the gesture is considered a major insult. It goes way back in Greek history to when fecal matter was pushed or propelled into the faces of prisoners of war. The gesture basically means "Eat shit."

The open hand gesture is insulting in Pakistan, in parts of Africa, and in several other countries. The Japanese used a similar gesture to insult the Koreans, except that they placed their thumb in the palm of their hands to form the gesture.

Not much needs to be said about the middle finger up gesture or the single-finger salute (Figure 22.9). It is certainly one of the most famous and well-known gestures of all. It's commonly referred to as the finger or the bird; when used as an insult, it's known as flipping the bird. In Latin it's called digitus impudicus, which translates to, "The indecent digit." Consider the fact that it's been used for more than 2,000 years, its meaning is understood globally. It is one gesture that *very* few people will make the mistake of using unintentionally.

When it comes to body language gestures in the communication process, the important thing to keep in mind is that what we *say*, we say with our *words*, *tonality*, and *body language*. As previously discussed in this book, our body language often conveys more than the words we use. At times, it can completely change—or even nullify—our words' meaning. And when our body language says the *opposite* of

Figure 22.9
Middle Finger Up Gesture
Graphic by Photos.com

our words, we come across as being completely incongruent. For example, if I claim that I'm not angry but my arms are crossed and my face is twisted into a scowl, my body language is speaking louder than my words—thereby making me much less credible.

There are countless gestures that mean something different in every culture—and there are many resources available for understanding these various multicultural gestures and their implications. Gestures have such a profound influence on communication that in our cross-cultural classes we caution attendees to *keep their fingers to themselves!*

Consider everything you read in this chapter. Almost every gesture using fingers is sure to offend someone, somewhere, at some time. As a rule of thumb (no pun intended!), it is best to avoid using any single finger as a gesture—unless you are *absolutely sure* it is appropriate in the country you are in. The only exception to this might be the single index finger pointed straight up to beckon a waiter, which is considered appropriate in many parts of the world.

It is also wise not to configure your fingers in any type of sign or signal. Open-handed gestures, with all fingers generally together, is usually considered the safest approach.

CHAPTER
23

Acronyms, Abbreviations, Analogies, Slang, and Sports Jargon

Does Anyone Know Where "Left Field" Is?

Acronyms and abbreviations create confusion and misunderstanding, no matter what culture you are from. This is only exacerbated by the fact that they are different for every industry and for every company. Before Circles Of Excellence will begin working with a new company, we ask for a list of that company's common acronyms and abbreviations. From ASP (average selling price) to YOY (year over year), business acronyms and abbreviations can be totally befuddling to the acronym un-savvy!

Acronyms and abbreviations are essentially a form of the old art of shorthand. Experts in shorthand were trained to understand the *language of shorthand*. But business professionals nowadays are expected to learn and understand the *language of business shorthand* without any formal training. Cross-cultural communication is challenging enough without having to worry about getting lost in the midst of a conversation due to undefined acronyms and abbreviations.

Communication is much easier, and much more understandable, when acronyms and abbreviations are *predefined, clarified, or eliminated if not needed*. This is helpful in *all* types of communication, regardless of the difference in cultures. It is best in written communication to provide a list of any acronyms and abbreviations that you're planning to use, along with a key or index defining their meaning. This will help you avoid any misunderstandings and also provide a reference point for those who don't understand the industry- or company-specific language.

Every business and profession, from accountants to zookeepers, has its own acronyms and abbreviations. The following are some examples of the more common ones used in the business world. Keep in mind that many of these will change, and be added to, as business cultures change. Chances are that once you learn these, it will be time to learn the new ones—because *change is the only constant*.

Common Business Acronyms in English

ASAP—as soon as possible

ASP—application service provider (company that provides services via a network)

B2B—business-to-business (companies that sell to other companies)

B2C—business-to-consumer (companies that sell to the general public)

BTW—by the way

CAD—computer-aided design (a design software for engineers and architects)

CAGR—compound annual growth rate (the cumulative interest rate banks use)

CEO—chief executive officer (head of the company)

CFO—chief financial officer (head of finance)

CIO—chief information officer (head of information technology)

CISO—chief information security officer (responsible for the security of information technology)

CMO—chief marketing officer (head of marketing)

COO—chief operating officer (head of operations)

CRM—customer relationship management (a system that manages all customer information)

CTO—chief technology officer (head of technology)

EDI—electronic data interchange (the set of standards used to exchange data)

EPS—earnings per share (the ratio between company profits and common shares)

ERP—enterprise resources planning (one system to organize all company information)

FIFO—first in, first out (used in accounting computer programs to ensure that what comes first is handled first)

FYI—for your information

GAAP—generally accepted accounting principles (the framework for financial accounting)

ICT—information and communications technology (encompasses all fields related to information technology)

IPO—initial public offering (the first company shares introduced on the stock market)

ISV—independent software vendor (a specialist in the production of software)

LIFO—last in, first out (confirms that what comes last is handled first)

LLC—limited liability company (a legal company where owners aren't personally liable)

MSRP—manufacturer's suggested retail price (company standardization or price)

MSA—master services agreement (an agreement detailing the services to be provided)

NDA—nondisclosure agreement (a contract to secure confidentiality of information)

NPV—net present value (a method to determine value on long-term investments)

OEM—original equipment manufacturer (the manufacturer of equipment that other companies will sell)

OTC—over-the-counter (the trade of stocks or derivatives directly between two parties)

P&L—profit and loss (a report that shows how revenues become profits)

POS—point of sale (where a sale was made)

RFP—request for proposal (a request for bids on a product or service)

ROI—return on investment (the ratio of money earned to total money invested)

ROS—return on sales (the ratio of money earned relative to total sales)

SAAS—Software As A Service (software developed on the Web and accessed via the Internet)

TCO—total cost of ownership (the estimate of all direct and indirect costs related to an expenditure)

TQM—total quality management (a strategy to lead an organization toward quality)

TSR—total shareholder return (the valuation determined by dividends and share price gains)

VC—venture capital (financing where some ownership is given up to an investor)

Common Business Abbreviations in English

a/c—bank account

A.G.M.—Annual General Meeting (usually of shareholders)

cc—carbon copy

CC—credit card

c.i.f.—cost, insurance, freight

c/o—care of (example: care of George Smith)

Co.—company

e.g.—for example (from the Latin *exempli gratia*)

FOB—free on board

FOC—free of charge

HQ—headquarters

Inc.—Incorporated (follows a corporation's company name)

Ltd.—Limited (follows the name of a legal company)

P.A.—personal assistant

PTO—paid time off

VAT—value-added tax

WP—word processing

Now for all you text-happy business professionals, there are literally *thousands* of abbreviations in text shorthand. Text is rapidly becoming the new e-mail, so it is absolutely essential that you make sure that the abbreviations you use are understood by the parties you use them with. Following are a few examples of abbreviations that are commonly used in business text. The good news is that the text shorthand is becoming a language in common around the world!

Common Business Text Abbreviations

10Q—thank you

121—one to one

AEAP—as early as possible

AFAIK—as far as I know

AFK—away from keyboard

@TEOTD—at the end of the day

BBL—be back later

BFN—bye for now

BRB—be right back

C/S—change of subject

COB—close of business

DBEYR—don't believe everything you read

EML—e-mail me later

GMAB—give me a break

HAGD—Have a good day

IMHO—in my humble opinion

NN2R—no need to respond

PCM—please call me

RTK—return to keyboard

S2US—speak to you soon

Analogies and metaphors are often very helpful to use in communication—that is, *as long as* they translate to mean the same thing when used in different cultures. An analogy is a likeness, or comparison, between things that are similar—yet different at the same time. I used an analogy in a prior chapter: "Relationships are like clay on a potter's wheel." This means that both need to be handled with care as they are molded and formed. This analogy is an example that explains, clarifies, and makes a concept easier to understand and remember. Analogies are particularly useful for important points or concepts that you want some-one to remember.

Business analogies are created in every country, culture, company, and industry. Salespeople, for instance, are often referred to as hunters, meaning they hunt for the customers, or as farmers, meaning they grow or expand the business with the customer. Sales terms around the analogy of fishing are commonly used; for example, "bait the hook" means to make a product or service enticing to the customer, and "cut bait" means that because the customer isn't buying, it's time to move on. In sales, the hunters, farmers, and fishermen are the ones who put the food on the table.

A metaphor is similar to an analogy; however, it is often a *figure of speech*, which has an implication of similarity and difference at the same time. For example, if I claim to be an "early bird," everyone would know I wasn't *literally* a bird (unless it was the 1960s in Britain, where the term was slang for a young woman). Since birds are awake in the very early morning, most would probably understand that the phrase meant I liked or tended to wake up early. Another example would be if I said that "I was a night owl." People would clearly understand that I wasn't an actual owl, and most would understand that I meant that I enjoyed staying up late at night.

Slang is another way of speaking that can leave someone from another culture completely bewildered. This is a casual, playful, humorous, and at times irreverent figure of speech that is used in place of standard terms. Slang has been used in every language since the beginning of time. Australians commonly refer to Australia as "OZ"; their friends are "mates," men are "blokes," and if something is very good, "it's bloody good!"

Slang usually comes and goes. However, some terms—like the word *cool*—have been lasting and universally used. *The biggest problem with slang in any language is that it is often taken literally by people from other cultures.* And there are often very humorous reactions and responses when this happens!

Common Slang in English

- **A dime a dozen**—something that is plentiful or very common
- **Aced it**—did something perfectly
- **Ante up**—give up what's due; give up the cash; give up the information
- **Ants in your pants**—nervous; fidgety; can't sit still (Can you imagine the picture this phrase creates when taken *literally?*)
- **As if**—wishful thinking about something that's unlikely to happen
- **Backseat driver**—someone who tells the driver how to drive
- **Bloke**—man or guy (typically used in the United Kingdom or Australia)
- **Bloody**—very (for example, "Bloody good!" This is typically used in British English.)
- **Brilliant**—wonderful; super; great (This is typically used in British English.)
- **Egghead**—brainy, but socially inept
- **Fat cat**—someone who has a lot of money (This often has people from other cultures wondering what a fat cat has to do with anything!)
- **Get it?**—Do you understand? (This phrase nearly always has people from other cultures asking, "Get what?")
- **Glued to your seat**—paying close attention
- **Go bananas**—go crazy; get very excited
- **Go postal**—go crazy; get violent
- **Goody two shoes**—someone who never does anything wrong or improper; someone who doesn't like to have a good time
- **Has a screw loose**—a bit crazy; not quite right
- **Hang out**—socialize with someone
- **Hit the road**—get going (from the famous song "Hit the Road Jack" by Ray Charles)
- **Hung up**—has a problem

- **Iffy**—uncertain
- **In a bind**—needs help
- **In a funk**—out of sorts; not feeling good
- **In someone's hair**—bothering someone (Imagine the picture this phrase creates when taken *literally!*)
- **In the doghouse**—in trouble (Often used by husbands after misbehaving at home!)
- **It went haywire**—something went wrong
- **Kooky**—weird
- **Laid back**—relaxed
- **Mate**—friend (This is typically used in British English.)
- **Nailed it**—same as "aced"; did it perfectly
- **Not my cup of tea**—not what I like; not my style
- **On cloud nine**—very happy (This phrase often causes people from other cultures to ask why we number our clouds!)
- **On the same wavelength**—thinking alike
- **Pig out**—eat a lot
- **Pipe down**—be quiet
- **Psyched**—excited; ready to start; ready to go
- **Raise the roof**—to show great enthusiasm or to get very upset
- **Rookie**—inexperienced; new at something
- **Screwed up**—made a mistake
- **Sitting duck**—vulnerable to attack
- **Stoked**—same as psyched: excited; ready to start; ready to go
- **Under the weather**—not at your best; not feeling as well as you could
- **Wimp**—someone without any strength or courage
- **Wishy-washy**—not consistent
- **Zilch**—nothing
- **Zip**—same as *zilch*; nothing
- **Zoned out**—not concentrating

Business slang and jargon vary from country to country, industry to industry, and company to company. It is wise to ensure that you either properly define all jargon or avoid it entirely. This is especially important when communicating multiculturally. Again, when people take business slang and jargon literally, some very humorous results can ensue!

Common Business Slang and Jargon in English

- **A bird's-eye view**—an overview; a look at the big picture
- **Act as if**—act like you can do or know something even if you're in doubt about it
- **All ears**—I'm listening; you have my full attention (Don't be surprised if someone from another culture responds by saying, "Your ears aren't all that big!")
- **Ammo**—short for *ammunition;* defense against something
- **At the end of the rope**—can't take it anymore; ready to quit; out of ideas; don't know what to do (This phrase has people from other cultures asking where the rope is!)
- **Back to the drawing board**—starting all over again (Be careful when using this in meetings, as this phrase often sends multicultural employees to the whiteboard at the back of the room.)
- **Bite the bullet**—do something that's unpleasant but necessary
- **Blue sky thinking**—unrealistic thoughts; ideas without practical application (This phrase will have multicultural employees believing that someone was thinking while looking up at a blue sky.)
- **Burnt out**—exhausted; tired of doing something
- **Cash cow**—a customer or client with money to spend (Don't be surprised if multicultural employees ask what selling cows has to do with anything!)
- **Cut a deal**—figure out a compromise to make the current situation work
- **Cut and dry**—clear; straightforward; understood, decided
- **Don't blow it**—don't ruin it; don't mess it up (This phrase often has multicultural employees thinking they can't blow their nose!)
- **Don't cut off your nose to spite your face**—don't do something that will create more harm than good; don't overreact in a self-destructive way (Can you imagine the picture this phrase creates when taken *literally?* Avoid ever using this phrase with people from the Asian cultures. They'll consider it offensive due to the concept of losing face, that is, losing someone's respect.)

- **Don't go off the deep end**—don't lose touch with reality (This phrase is often associated with swimming to people from other cultures.)
- **Don't knock it**—don't criticize it (This phrase usually means "don't knock on the door" to multicultural employees.)
- **Drink our own champagne**—to use the same product or service business that is sold to customers
- **EYODF (eat your own dog food)**—if our product is good enough for our customers, it's good enough for us
- **End user perspective**—to think like the customer and see things like they do
- **Get your ducks in a row**—getting ready; organizing things efficiently and effectively (The interpretations of this phrase by people from other cultures can be hilarious. It's not uncommon to hear them say, "All the geese are in a line" or "The pigeons are all straight!")
- **Hands on**—requiring active involvement and participation
- **Hang in there**—stick with it; you can do it
- **Heads up**—pay attention
- **I have your back**—to cover for or protect someone
- **It was a piece of cake**—it was easy
- **Land and expand**—making a small sale and expanding to provide add-on products or services
- **No-brainer**—requires no thought
- **Pitch in**—help others
- **Pushing the envelope**—stretching the limits; going beyond what is normal (This phrase often gets the response, "When will I receive it?" from multicultural employees.)
- **Put a Band-Aid on it**—a temporary fix or an incomplete solution to a problem
- **Put it in the parking lot** or **park it**—used in meetings to set something aside for later discussion, that is, "parking" a topic to come back to it at a later time (This phrase might have multicultural employees thinking that someone needs to move his or her car.)
- **Put it on the back burner**—come back to that topic later
- **Revved up**—ready to go; excited to start
- **Roll out the red carpet**—treat someone like royalty

- **Run it up the flagpole**—try out an idea to see if others will agree (Many people don't know *what* to think about this phrase.)
- **Strike three or third strike**—the last chance
- **Thinking outside the box**—creative thinking; not limiting your thoughts to what's expected
- **The helicopter view**—an overview; the big picture (like a bird's-eye view) (This phrase might initiate the response, "When did you take the helicopter ride?" from multicultural employees.)
- **Table it**—*In the United States:* to put something away and come back to it later; *in the United Kingdom:* to do something right now (Note the completely opposite meanings—which, of course, can cause some confusion!)
- **Time is money**—don't waste your time
- **Top of the line**—the very best there is
- **Up for grabs**—anyone can have it; it's there for the taking
- **Upsell**—similar to *land and expand;* upselling new or different products and services
- **Walking on eggshells**—being extremely careful (This makes for a lot of broken eggs!)
- **What's the angle**—what's the scheme, approach, or plan to a given situation?

Although there are many more examples of business slang and jargon, I will now "table it" U.S. style and move on to business sports jargon.

Analogies made to sports, and the use of sports jargon in the United States, is so popular and so entwined throughout business communication that they are nearly indistinguishable from each other. In fact, my company has developed entire training programs on the topic of sports analogies in business. And as with all slang and jargon, sports jargon will frequently be taken literally. I can't count the times we've had someone in our classes ask, "Where is left field . . . *really?!*"

Common Business Sports Jargon in English

- **At the 100-yard line**—nearly ready to close the deal; close to succeeding (like with the phrase "Where is left field?" this will have multicultural employees asking, "Exactly where *is* the 100-yard line?")
- **Ballpark figure**—a rough estimate of the cost

- **Batting average**—the number of successful efforts in relation to the number of attempts
- **Big league or major league**—important; high-ranking; influential; highly paid
- **Blitz**—a powerful attack or act
- **Front line**—in the leading position with the most risk and the greatest reward
- **Hole in one**—immediate and perfectly executed success
- **Home run**—got everything you wanted
- **Home stretch**—approaching the end of something
- **Let's huddle**—let's put our heads together and decide what to do (This phrase will get the puzzled response of, "Let's *what?*" from multicultural employees.)
- **Monday morning quarterback**—someone uninvolved who tells you how something *should have been done*
- **Off base**—incorrect (Avoid using this in the Middle Eastern cultures; a jihad is sometimes referred to as a base.)
- **On base**—correct; or it can mean that you've taken the first step in a new venture (Again, avoid using with Middle Eastern cultures for the same reason as above.)
- **Out in left field**—someone who doesn't know what he or she is talking about; something that doesn't make sense (This phrase *really* doesn't make sense to people from other cultures, and often has them looking over their left shoulder!)
- **Out of the ballpark**—a great accomplishment
- **Put on your game face**—look like you're ready
- **Score big**—make it profitable; be successful
- **Slam dunk**—perfectly executed and easily done
- **Step up to the plate**—do it
- **Touch base**—to get in touch or connect with each other; to find out what is going on (Again, avoid using in the term *base* with Middle Eastern cultures.)
- **We creamed them**—we beat them by a lot
- **We'll punt**—we'll take a gamble and see if it works; we'll stop for now and try it a different way

- **Whole 9 yards**—a decisive victory
- **You can't hit the ball if you don't swing**—you have to take action

Along with acronyms, slang, and jargon, we should also say something about humor and jokes between cultures. A little humor can open many doors, and every culture appreciates a good joke. However, unless the joke originated in someone's native language, it may not translate well. In addition, the concept of what different people consider humorous varies from one culture to the next. Indeed, the senses of humor between the English-speaking countries of the United Kingdom, the United States, Canada, and Australia are uniquely distinct. As a professional speaker, I only use humor and jokes that have been previously approved by natives of the country or culture to whom I'm speaking. When there is a multicultural audience, I will avoid any humor or joke that my audience members won't universally understand. It's best to avoid using jokes entirely than to be looking at a group of expressionless (or worse, offended) faces!

For the most effective cross-cultural communication, and especially for group presentations, it is usually best to *eliminate* any acronyms, abbreviations, analogies, and jargon that other cultures are likely not to understand. I frequently advise my fellow speakers or presenters to ask themselves, "If I didn't know what this term meant, what would I *think* it meant?" Chances are, even if you didn't take it literally, you would be thoroughly confused. If it doesn't *logically make sense* in the context that it is used to you, it clearly won't make sense to someone from another culture, so it's wisest to eliminate it.

CHAPTER
24

Global Etiquette Tips

What All Cultures Appreciate—No Need to Reinvent the Wheel!

Cultural etiquette, politeness, and good manners are passed down through societies from generation to generation. *Etiquette* refers to the cultural guidelines for what is appropriate or inappropriate and polite or impolite. It gives a culture structure, integrity, grace, and finesse—all of which are uniquely adapted from one culture to another. Fortunately, simple business and social etiquette are often based on basic common sense. Although etiquette styles and fads may come and go, the fundamentals of global etiquette remain essentially the same.

The following tips on *what to do* and *what to avoid* will help you engage in successful global business and social interactions. Although not all tips necessarily apply to all cultures, they will help to avoid embarrassing faux pas and guide you toward establishing quality relationships and friendships.

What to Do

- **Show respect.** The most important of the global etiquette tips is to show respect for what is important to another person and his or her culture. This includes respecting the various cultural

179

distinctions that make us all unique and individual. Although cultural conditioning has deep roots, *respect is universally understood*—and is an essential step in bridging the cultural gap.

- **Show you care.** Be proactive and learn about what's important to the cultures you visit or interact with. This will help you win friendships and develop business relationships. Selling a skyscraper means nothing to someone who is concerned with how many cows will fit in a barn.

- **Strike a balance.** Find the comfortable *middle ground* between your culture and that which you're visiting or working with. No one expects you to be just like him or her, nor would that be congruent. Be yourself and adapt to develop rapport in a way that works for all concerned.

- **Learn the rules and laws.** Don't think that you can simply do things "your way" without any consideration for important cultural differences. For example, it is illegal for a woman to drive a car in Saudi Arabia, so don't plan on renting one if you are a female! Sometimes when in Rome, it's necessary to do as the Romans. Although you may not agree with or support some of these, it's best to learn—and then follow—the customs and laws of the countries you visit.

- **Know your geography.** There is nothing more embarrassing than not knowing the *exact* location of the country you are visiting or the locality of its neighboring countries and surrounding areas. In addition, it's advisable to learn something about the country's general environment, terrain, and climate, all of which will serve as good points of discussion later on.

- **Mind your manners.** What is polite in one culture may not be considered so in another, so know your manners for the countries you visit. Table manners are a good example of these differences. For example, it is proper in the United States to keep the left hand in your lap when eating. However, most of Europe considers it polite to keep both hands on the table, a tradition that dates back centuries to when people thought someone might be concealing a weapon if his hand was in his lap. Table manners in the Middle East differ from both the U.S. and European manners. There, the left hand is considered the *unclean hand* and should never come in contact with your food, plate, or utensils. Many European and Latin American cultures also believe that it is impolite to discuss business at meals. Bottom line: Be prepared when it comes to manners.

- **Know the appropriate attire**. It's important to know what is appropriate to wear for both business and social occasions when you visit other countries. Formality in business attire varies a great deal from country to country. When in doubt, it's always best to err on the side of formality. In general, many of the European, Asian Pacific, and Latin American cultures tend to be more formal than the United States, Canada, and Australia.

- **Learn the protocol**. Since professional protocol varies from culture to culture, you'll want to learn the expected protocol for the cultures with whom you work. For example, the Asian, European, and Latin American cultures tend to have more decorum and procedures, as well as great respect for elders, seniority, title, and rank. It's important to know the business hierarchical structure and the role that status plays, in addition to how the culture relates to time, security, and risk (all topics that are covered in prior chapters).

- **Know how to address people**. The practice of using first names, surnames, titles, university degrees, or religious designations varies from country to country. In some countries, such as China, the family name comes first, whereas people in parts of Latin America use three or more names plus their family names.

- **Learn a few native words *and* the correct pronunciations**. It's always polite to know a few words in the language of another culture; however, it can be very challenging to master pronunciation in another language, even for adept multilingual speakers. If you are unclear about how to pronounce something, *especially* someone's name, just ask what the proper pronunciation is. Even if the letters are the same as in your own language, they may be pronounced differently. For example, in Italian the letter c is pronounced as "ch," whereas in Spanish and English, it's pronounced as "s" or "k." It's better to check and get it right than to inadvertently offend someone.

- **Clearly enunciate and speak slower**. Speak clearly and slightly slower—about 20 percent slower—when communicating across linguistic borders. However, despite what many people tend to do, there's no need to speak louder. Multilingual speakers may be cross-translating, but they aren't deaf!

- **Define acronyms, slang, and jargon.** Define, clarify, or eliminate any acronyms, abbreviations, slang, and jargon that other cultures may not understand. You want to avoid the odds that they will create misunderstanding, confusion, or even be taken *literally!*

- **Be careful with humor.** As discussed in the previous chapter, every culture appreciates humor and a good joke. However, some jokes don't translate very well between cultures. Furthermore, even the sense of humor between the English-speaking countries of the United Kingdom, the United States, Canada, and Australia differ greatly. It's preferable to avoid using humor and jokes than to be the only one laughing!

- **Know the appropriate greetings.** Greetings are as diverse as the cultures themselves. There are handshakes, kisses, hugs, and bows—and they come in all shapes and sizes. Handshakes range from gentle to firm to "Texan" (extra firm!). They can have only one pump or multiple pumps, and they can be frequent (given upon meeting and departing) or infrequent (given only when initially meeting). Kisses on the cheek are common in much of Europe, Latin America, and the Middle East. Kisses may be given between both men and women or between same sexes only. There may be one kiss, or four or more, depending on where you are. A hug, or abrazo, is typical among male friends in much of Latin America. In many parts of Asia, a bow is part of the standard greeting. In Japan the higher the person's stature, the lower you bow. So, in summary, know your greetings.

- **Learn the business card exchange.** Is it one handed or two handed, and do the cards need to be translated or not? Although single-handed business card exchanges are probably the most common, a two-handed exchange (where the card is held between the thumb and forefingers with both hands) is the rule in much of Asia. In Japan, the business card exchange is referred to as *meishi* and is done with great respect.

- **Balance tonality and body language.** Although you don't want to be overly expressive with your tonality and body language, it's equally important to be expressive *enough* for the cultures with whom you interact. The same goes for the use of emotion in communication. Many of the Latin American cultures freely show emotion, whereas the United Kingdom and many northern

European countries tend to show very little. The rule is straightforward here: Follow the cues of the culture with which you are communicating.

- **Have good eye contact.** Making good eye contact is necessary with all cultures. However, you want to keep in mind that some cultures are more comfortable holding the gaze longer than others. In parts of Asia and some Latin American cultures, the length of the eye contact is determined by status and seniority. It's not appropriate to have prolonged eye contact with someone more senior than yourself. There was even a California court case where the judge held a Hispanic American in contempt of court for not maintaining eye contact. It was later understood that this was done out of respect for the judge.

- **Understand formality.** Determine in advance whether a culture is inclined to be more casual or formal in its general communication and business style. For instance, the European, Asian, and Latin American cultures tend to be more formal, whereas the U.S., Canadian, and Australian cultures tend to be less formal. Follow the culture's cues in both your verbal and written communication.

- **Balance business and relationships.** Relationships can take longer to develop in many countries and cultures. Avoid being overly anxious to begin business discussions and be prepared for some social interaction and small talk. Follow the lead of the culture with which you are engaging to build rapport.

- **Balance process and results.** Everyone is clearly looking for results; that's why you're engaged in an interaction in the first place. However, many cultures—including the Asian, European, Latin American, and Middle Eastern cultures—place as much emphasize on *how* the results are achieved as the results themselves. In other words, the process is just as important as the outcome here, so have respect for the time it takes to achieve your collective goal.

- **Ask valid questions and *listen*.** *All* cultures appreciate honest questions. Most people are quite happy to answer questions or to discuss their country or culture. Be a good listener and allow the responding party to finish his or her answer without interrupting or beginning to walk away. Remember: *We have two ears and one mouth for a reason!*

- **Understand common space.** The level of comfort in common space varies around the world. In highly populated countries, people stand very close together and "touch without touching"—as on the subways in Japan. People from the Middle East are more comfortable standing closer together (nearly nose to nose) when communicating than are those from Western cultures. If someone ever seems uncomfortably close to you, try leaning slightly toward that person and he or she will likely move back a bit. Don't back away yourself, because this will cause the other person to move toward you—and you may find yourself in a backward dance!

- **Respect time differences.** As discussed in a previous chapter, various cultures relate to the concept of time differently. Although the British, northern European, and Asian cultures are very punctual, many southern European, Latin American, and Middle Eastern cultures have a more flexible approach to time. Another factor to keep in mind is that most countries outside the United States use a 24-hour clock (what is known in the United States as military time) instead of the 12-hour clock. For example, 7:00 PM would be written as 19:00.

- **Understand dates.** Dates are written differently in various parts of the world. Although not a complete list, it's good to keep the following general guidelines in mind:

  1. ISO 8601 International Standard: year-month-day, 2013–03–31

  2. Asia Pacific: year-month-day, 2013.03.31

  3. Europe, Australia, New Zealand, Canada: day-month-year, 31/03/2013

  4. The United States: month-day-year, 03–31–2013

- **Know the common Celsius temperature and Metric system conversions.** Most countries outside the United States, including Canada, use these. It's important to know the basics when traveling.

  1. 0 degrees Celsius equals 32 degrees Fahrenheit

  2. 1 kilometer equals 0.621 miles

  3. 1 liter equals 0.264 gallons

- **Honor your word.** This is important to every culture, but especially in the Asian and Latin American cultures, where your word, trust, and honor are the most important things in a business relationship. This extends to all inferred, verbal, and written communication as well.

- **Finally, *enjoy yourself!*** This might sound a bit difficult after hearing about all these "rules," but it *is* possible—and will do a great deal to help you! Do your homework, then relax and connect at the human culture level. If you enjoy working with or visiting other cultures, they are likely to enjoy the same with you.

What to Avoid

- **Using rude hand gestures:** As discussed in a previous chapter, unless you are counting on your fingers in the fashion of the country you are visiting, avoid any hand gestures that you think could be potentially offensive to other cultures. It is very difficult to recover if you unintentionally offend someone with a gesture.

- **Discussing religion:** It's safest to avoid touching on the topic of religion, unless the other person brings it up first. Whatever you are discussing—Taoism, Hinduism, or Catholicism—there is a chance that religious prejudice could be a problematic topic.

- **Discussing politics:** It's safest to keep politics, global affairs, and even a country's economic condition out of the conversation— again, unless the other person brings it up first. There are often a lot of hot buttons around these topics.

- **Discussing sensitive topics:** Avoid bringing up any current issues (wars, terrorism, political or environmental embarrassment, etc.) that could be potentially sensitive in the countries you are visiting or doing business with. And make sure you research this shortly before your departure date so that you're aware of recent events.

- **Unintentionally causing embarrassment:** People are embarrassed by different things in different cultures. Doing your research on the potentially embarrassing factors of specific cultures beforehand will help you avoid this. Causing unintentional embarrassment can have negative consequences the same way as unintentionally offending someone with inappropriate gestures. For instance, most members of the Asian cultures are made uncomfortable by anything that may put someone on the spot or that shows them in a negative light due to the concept of loss of face. In contrast, the Scandinavian cultures tend to be self-effacing when receiving compliments, so keep your compliments subdued.

- **Making inappropriate actions:** Whistling, chewing gum, smoking, or blowing your nose (especially in a handkerchief that you put in your pocket) may be offensive in many places, including parts of Europe, Asia, and the Middle East. Chewing gum is banned in Singapore unless it is for therapeutic use. So, like other things, find out what is appropriate.

- **Asking personal questions:** As discussed in a previous chapter, there is a big difference in what various cultures consider to be public or private information. When in doubt, it's safest to *wait* to ask personal questions (about family, etc.) until someone poses these kinds of questions to you first.

- **Asking superficial questions:** As discussed in a previous chapter, making questions such as, "Hi, how are you?" part of a greeting can seem superficial and meaningless to some cultures. It's best to ask questions that introduce a topic you *genuinely* want to have a dialogue about, including queries about how someone is doing.

- **Touching:** Many cultures, including the U.S., southern European, and some Latin American cultures, are comfortable with back pats or having an arm, elbow, or shoulder touched. However, this might be uncomfortable and inappropriate for someone from the British, northern Europeans, and Asian cultures. If, on the other hand, someone touches you or links arms while walking, it would be inappropriate to back away. Remember the picture of President George W. Bush and Saudi Crown Prince Abdullah walking hand in hand in Chapter 9! Follow the culture's lead when it comes to touching.

- **Being overly assertive:** Some European, Asian, and Latin American cultures perceive someone who is overly assertive as *aggressive*. It is wise to be moderately assertive and show that you have the patience to develop the necessary trust and rapport for successful business relationships.

- **Appearing self-important:** Although the United States is known to prize self-confidence and the entrepreneurial spirit, some cultures—including many in Europe and Asia—prefer a more humble, group-oriented approach in their communication style. Rather than concentrating on "I," they are more focused on "we."

They value humility and modesty, so avoid being boastful and don't "blow your own horn"—or others might peg you as arrogant.

- **Showing the soles of your shoes:** This may seem like a strange one, but showing the sole of your shoe is offensive in many cultures, including the Middle East and parts of Asia. For this reason, it is wise for men not to rest their foot on their knee, as it would likely result in their sole pointing at someone. Also be mindful not to raise your foot at the ankle if your feet are on the ground or your legs are crossed, as this could also result in pointing your foot at someone.

- **Touching your head:** Some cultures, including the Indian culture and many Asian cultures, believe that the head and area around the head are sacred, so minimize scratching your head or playing with your hair and ears. It can be annoying in *any* culture when someone does this habitually.

- **Saying "no":** Many cultures, including the Asian and some Latin American cultures, consider saying "no" directly to be impolite. If pushed for a firm "no," they will become very uncomfortable. When possible, it's advisable to use *who, what, when, where,* and *why* questions rather than, *yes/no* questions with these cultures (see Chapter 17).

When it comes to cultural etiquette, no one expects perfection. Awareness is always the first step, so stop, look, and listen. Remaining aware will likely help you figure out most of what you need to know.

Area-Specific Cultural Clues, Do's, and Taboos

For Successful Multicultural Navigation

As previously discussed in the book, numerous countries and cultures often have shared characteristics that are based on the origin of their mother tongue languages, environment, climate, and ethnic background, among other things. This chapter highlights 21 of the most important *area- and language-specific characteristics* or traits that various countries and cultures have in common.

Although not all of the cultural clues necessarily apply to every country in a given area or region, they are generally the case for the majority. That being said, keep in mind there are as many differences between the individual countries and cultures as there are commonalities.

For the purpose of simplification, the following cultural clues are organized into six categories that reflect material previously discussed in Chapter 12. The clues start with the cultures with less melody in their languages—those cultures that tend to communicate with a strong emphasis on the words that people use (*what* is said). They progressively continue to end with the cultures with more melody in their languages, those that tend to communicate by emphasizing the tonality and body language that people use (*how* it is said).

The Germanic, Scandinavian, and Nordic Cultures

1. These cultures have firm handshakes (one or two pumps are appropriate) when arriving and departing. It is appropriate to shake hands with every person present. Cheek kissing is rare and usually takes place only between friends.

2. People from these cultures may initially seem stiff and overly serious; however, they tend to warm up as the relationship develops. There is little use for superficial inquiries or observations, and it can take longer to cultivate relationships with these individuals.

3. These cultures tend to keep their personal information quite private during business communications, so avoid asking personal questions until they are asked of you. They greatly respect and value a sense of privacy, so don't become too familiar too soon.

4. First names are commonly used in business relationships. However, if you are introduced using surnames (Mr., Ms., or the equivalent in the relevant language), then use the surnames. Some of these cultures answer the phone simply by saying their last name and nothing more. For example, I would answer the phone by saying, "Cotton"—that's it.

5. Spatial relationships are a full arm's length apart, and there is very little physical touching or back patting. Members of this culture appreciate good posture, so it is important to stand upright. They generally emphasize *what* is said (the words) more than *how* it is said (tonality and body language), so they consequently use less tonality and body language in their overall communication. When they do use it, it is much more subtle, so be more subtle with yours as well.

6. This culture's business communication tends to be less expressive and emotional, with fewer tonal range highs and lows than found in many cultures. To build rapport, it's advisable to be less expressive and emotional with your tonality as well.

7. Eye contact during introductions is serious and direct, and it should be maintained as long as the person is addressing you. Facial expressions are also serious and focused.

8. These cultures consider punctuality to be very important; however, the business pace is unrushed. Business is taken seriously and is carefully planned, well organized, structured, and more formal than in some other cultures.

9. They treat business meetings as important occasions. According to business protocol, the eldest or highest-ranking person usually enters the room first. They also reserve humor and jokes for socializing. Refrain from interrupting others, and allow each speaker to make his or her point before responding. Don't slouch, lean on furniture, or rest your foot on your knee.

10. Make sure your communication is well organized, direct, precise, detailed, and to the point. Very little small talk is necessary, and conversations focus mainly on matters of substance and genuine interest.

11. These cultures appreciate humility and modesty, so they often minimize or even deny compliments. Don't be overly complimentary to anyone; it may make them uncomfortable. Avoid being perceived as self-important or boastful. Do not "blow your own horn"—or others might see you as egocentric or arrogant.

12. It is considered impolite to open a closed door before knocking. Although the open door style of management is becoming more popular, take heed to knock before entering a manager's office if the door is closed.

13. These cultures pay attention to the business hierarchy and do not freely share information among the various levels of the same organization. However, this is beginning to change a bit among younger generations.

14. Flexibility and spontaneity are not prominent traits in these business cultures. They therefore don't consider qualities such as risk taking or challenging the rules and authority to be desirable characteristics.

15. The U.S. wave for "good-bye" (palm out, moving side to side) means "no" in these cultures. To wave good-bye, bounce your hand up and down at the wrist.

16. Do not use the OK sign, because it is considered very rude and obscene. Keep your hands out of your pockets, and avoid chewing gum when conversing.

17. It is acceptable to beckon a waiter by pointing with the index finger up; this is not an offensive use of the index finger. However, do not beckon anyone by curling the index finger. Instead, turn your hand so that the palm faces down and make a scratching motion.

18. Hitting the table with fists with the thumbs tucked in means "good luck" and is in no way a sign of impatience.

19. These cultures eat "continental style" with the fork in the left hand and the knife in the right. It is polite to keep both hands on the table while eating; however, they are comfortable if you choose to keep one hand in your lap.

20. Always wait for your host to begin drinking at business or social dinners. Toasting is frequent at meals, and the host usually makes the first toast. This is done by lifting the glass, making eye contact with everyone around, and saying the toast in the relevant language (for example, "Prost!").

21. When dining in a restaurant, it is not uncommon for strangers to join your table; however, there is no need to converse with them.

The Asia/Pacific, Chinese, and Japanese Cultures

1. Many members of Asian cultures have three names, the first usually being the family name. This is important to know when addressing someone, especially in e-mail. Very often, Westerners e-mail Asians using their family name thinking that it is their first name. As a result, many Asians have started putting their family name last, which makes it even more confusing for Western cultures. Surnames (Mr., Ms., or the equivalent in the language of the culture) are still frequently used in some cultures, including China and South Korea.

2. Handshaking is common and is often accompanied by a slight nod or bow. In Japan, how low you bow is determined by the seniority and age of the person you are meeting. A light, rather gentle grip is appropriate for handshakes. A very firm handshake suggests aggression, although people from these cultures may surprise you with a firm handshake, because they are quick to adopt Western habits with Western cultures.

3. Dual-language business cards are recommended and are offered with both hands, grasped between thumb and forefingers. Your

title or position should always be on the card. Upon receiving a card, read it carefully and keep it near you for future reference. Never casually toss it in a pocket or handbag. Members of these cultures believe that you must treat business cards with great care because they represent one's identity and station in life.

4. These cultures emphasize giving great respect to the elderly. To them, age is synonymous with wisdom and experience. Speak to elders first, hold doors open for them, rise when they enter the room, give up your seat if need be, and remove glasses when addressing them. Seniority, rank, and hierarchy are very important. Senior people typically begin the greeting first, so greet the oldest, most senior person before any others. During group introductions, line up your own group according to seniority with the senior person at the head of the line.

5. Asian cultures are punctual, formal, polite, and structured when it comes to business. Tradition is at the heart of nearly all Asian cultures. For example, Korea has a 5,000-year history and has been invaded more than 500 times; however, its traditions remain intact. The personal side of a business relationship is extremely important. Relationships take longer to develop, and trust and loyalty are essential.

6. Good eye contact is appropriate, although it won't be prolonged. Asian cultures often avert their eyes to avoid the intimidation that long, frequent eye contact might create. Conspicuous eye blinking is considered impolite when conversing and can be perceived as a sign of disrespect or boredom.

7. Many Asian cultures have large populations and out of necessity are required to stand very close together on public transportation, in lines, and so on. As a result, these cultures have learned to "touch without touching" when in crowded areas. However, they tend to stand farther apart than many other cultures when engaged in business interactions.

8. These cultures are apt to be more process-oriented in business than many Western cultures, which tend to be more results-oriented. In Asian cultures, the style and how something is done is equally as important as what is done.

9. Politeness, humility, patience, harmony, and grace are appreciated and respected. Avoid using any excessively demonstrative

behavior or raising your voice too loud. It is considered impolite to yawn or display an open mouth in these cultures.

10. These are *not* "touching" cultures, so avoid back patting, putting an arm around someone's shoulders, hugs, or holding hands. However, friends of the same sex may occasionally walk hand in hand in some Asian cultures.

11. Posture and balance are very important. Avoid slouching or putting your feet on desks and chairs. While seated, it is customary to place the hands in the lap and not fidget or wiggle the legs.

12. Never cross your legs with the foot resting on the knee. It is considered disrespectful and may result in unintentionally pointing the sole of your shoe at someone. It is a serious insult to show the soles of your shoes or to point your feet at anyone in most of the Asian cultures. It is customary to remove shoes before entering carpeted rooms in offices or homes if visiting or working in Asian cultures.

13. When pointing to something, do so with an open hand rather than one or two fingers, because beckoning with the index is considered very rude. To beckon someone, extend the hand with the palm downward and make a scratching motion. Do not snap your fingers, wink, whistle, or blow your nose in a handkerchief and put in a pocket or handbag. Certain Asian cultures perceive these actions as very impolite.

14. These cultures prefer more indirect communication and hate to disappoint or disagree. As a result, they rarely say "no" directly. Instead they may say, "Maybe," or "That could be difficult"—which usually means "no." It's best to phrase your questions to avoid a direct yes or no answer. Using open-ended questions, such as *who, what, when, where, why,* and *how* questions, is very helpful with Asian cultures. And instead of saying, "no" yourself, directly wave the palm of your hand, facing outward like a windshield wiper, next to your face.

15. Don't be alarmed if there are frequent periods of silence in your dinner or business conversations; silence is a sign of politeness and contemplation. Be especially careful not to interrupt someone while he or she is speaking during a conversation. When making presentations for Asian groups or audiences, don't be surprised when they are very silent, serious, and attentive. Western cultures often think they are doing something wrong when they get so

little reaction or feedback from Asian audiences when, in fact, they are doing something right!

16. The Asian cultures see patience as a virtue. Although decisions often come from the top, they are made by consensus after considerable discussion. Consequently, negotiations and the decision-making process can take more time. This contrasts sharply to the Western decision-making style where one person frequently makes an important choice—and can therefore do so much more quickly.

17. Asian cultures are very careful to give group or team credit rather than taking personal credit, because it is rare that only one person is solely responsible for accomplishing something. It's undesirable to stand out as an individual in these cultures and can cause loss of face in front of peers and business colleagues. This is clearly very different from many Western cultures, where individual credit and praise is something people actively seek out.

18. Avoid singling anyone out or causing any type of embarrassment, because this will result in loss of face. In Asian cultures, someone who has a "good face" (simply referred to as face) has a good reputation with his or her peers, business colleagues, community, and so on. *Having face is a bankable notion that is literally a statement of a person's value.* If someone makes a mistake or does something wrong, then that person has lost face—and his or her reputation has been damaged as a result (no face). *Saving face* is an action where the person is able to prove that he or she was not wrong or that the wrongdoing was very minimal. *Giving face* is the concept of offering public recommendation, compliments, approval, or praise to a person, group, or organization. Asians not only think about their own face; they think about the face of the groups and organizations to which they belong. This orientation contrasts with members of typical Western cultures, who are concerned more with losing individual face. *Lending face* occurs when a person has no face or recognized reputation and is required to seek out and "borrow face" from someone willing to lend it. This is often necessary for a foreigner doing business in Asia. The concept of face is so important that in traditional Asian families, children are taught at a very young age to care about face, because their face is also their family's face.

19. Asian cultures are typically gift-giving cultures. You want to keep individual gifts modest, and often a gift is also offered to the group or organization with whom you are meeting. The ritual of gift giving is typically more important than the value of the gift, and overly extravagant gifts might be considered a form of bribery. Never give a clock, handkerchief, white flowers, scissors, or knives as a gift, because these have negative connotations associated with them. Make sure your gifts are culturally sensitive for the specific country, and avoid black and white because both of these colors are associated with death. Some cultures, including Japan, consider gifts in the amounts of four to be unlucky. Many countries, such as South Korea, Singapore, and Malaysia, have several different ethnic groups, so the gift-giving protocol will change according to the group. For the most part, it's polite to give and receive gifts with *both* hands; however, in cultures where the left hand is considered unclean, the gift should be given with the right hand only. It is the way of these cultures to initially decline a gift one or two times as a matter of etiquette. Some cultures may not open the gift until later, so they won't be perceived as impatient.

20. There tend to be fewer young men or women in the higher levels of the business hierarchy in these cultures. Age is synonymous with wisdom, experience, rank, and seniority when it comes to promotion, and women typically haven't been in business as long as men. Although this is changing with the younger generation, it is still quite common for a longtime employee to be rewarded by promotion based on loyalty, rather than ability, since Asian business cultures value loyalty highly.

21. When dining in these cultures, it's best to follow the "When in Rome, do as the Romans" motto, because habits and customs vary greatly between the individual countries. The dining experience is an opportunity to develop a relationship further and create enhanced rapport. Sharing meals is vital to building friendships and social relationships that foster trust and understanding in business relationships.

The English Language Cultures

1. Although many of the original inhabitants of the United States, Canada, Australia, and other English-speaking cultures may have initially come from England, there are as many differences as there

are similarities between these countries. And when you take all of the former British colonies into consideration, the differences become even more apparent. Don't be fooled into thinking that because these countries have a language in common that their business or social styles are the same—because this is not the case.

2. The British clearly have the most formal and conservative social styles and business practices of all the English language cultures. They also tend to be the most understated, reserved, and private about their personal lives. Status and rank are more important in the United Kingdom than in most of the other cultures.

3. Handshakes are the most firm in the United States, moderately firm in Canada and Australia, and lighter and rather gentle in the United Kingdom. They are also generally given upon arriving and departing in all the countries. In the United States, it is optional to shake hands at social events, and people may simply greet you with a casual "Hello" or "Hi."

4. In most of these cultures, hugging, kissing, and touching are usually reserved for family members and close friends. The exception is French-speaking Canadians, who may choose to use the French custom of kisses on the cheek.

5. First names are commonly used in these cultures. However, if someone introduces himself or herself to you using a title or surname—as is often the case in the United Kingdom—then use that person's title and surname until you are invited to use his or her first name. Using titles based on royal designations is always expected in the United Kingdom. In other cultures, professional titles are typically used when making new introductions. For example, you would introduce Judge Jim Harper to Dr. Marion Allen. Of course, it is up to you whether to use your professional title or not if you are introducing yourself.

6. Keep your distance when conversing with people from these cultures. If they feel you are standing too close, they will likely back away without even thinking about it. You shouldn't consider this to be any type of insult; it is simply an unconscious reaction to establish the distance with which they are comfortable.

7. Body language varies among these cultures. The U.S. Americans and Australians tend to use body language more frequently than do people from the United Kingdom and Canada; however, the

tendencies vary widely in different areas of each country. For example, French Canadians will usually incorporate more body language than Western Canadians, where there is more of a British influence. Avoid the V for victory gesture in Australia. As mentioned in a previous chapter, former U.S. President George H.W. Bush offended Australians when he used this gesture with his palm facing toward him, which, in essence, meant, "Up yours!"—the equivalent of the middle finger up.

8. All these cultures are generally uncomfortable with same-sex touching, especially between males. The exception is French-speaking Canada, where they may use more of the body language associated with the French culture.

9. Citizens of the English-speaking countries generally expect you to be independent and take care of yourself. Personal initiative, ambition, and action are all desirable traits. The business environment is openly competitive, and hard work is valued. Direct contact with upper levels and senior management is not uncommon. Personal lives, family, and friendships tend not to influence business outcomes as much as in some other cultures.

10. Members of these cultures appreciate when you share different or strong opinions, even if they don't agree with you. You'll need to put your reservations aside, because there will be plenty of information exchanged. Don't be afraid to be direct and specific, speak your mind, or ask for help. Although it is clearly not polite to purposefully insult anyone, simply apologize and move on if it happens unintentionally.

11. Tonality in communication fluctuates considerably between these cultures. The United Kingdom is the most moderate in their use of expressive tonality, but tendencies will vary greatly in different areas of Canada, Australia, and the United States.

12. All the English-speaking cultures generally prefer directness to indirectness in their communication. When they say "yes" or "no," they mean precisely that; and the word *maybe* actually means that "it *might* happen." It does not mean "no," as would be the case in the cultures who hesitate to say "no" directly, like many of the Asian Pacific cultures.

13. Be aware of the English-English and the thousands of different word meanings between American and British English. For

example, "to table something" in the United States means "to set it aside or discuss it at another time." In the United Kingdom, it means exactly the opposite—"to take care of something or discuss something immediately."

14. It is important to have an expert translator do all the multinational translating and advertising for translations between British and American English. There are many word, spelling, nuance, and acronym differences between these countries.

15. Punctuality is very important for business meetings and appointments in all of these cultures. It is appropriate to call if you will be more than 5 to 10 minutes late—and then to apologize for your lateness upon arrival.

16. Meetings and appointments need to be scheduled well in advance and are organized and structured with the desired outcome in mind. They generally have concrete objectives laid out for developing a plan, making a decision, or negotiating an agreement.

17. These cultures are typically tolerant and open-minded and appreciate a sense of self-control. Excessive anger, emotional outbursts, shouting, or rash behavior is deemed inappropriate in business meetings.

18. It is impolite to interrupt someone while they are speaking. If you must do so, politely say, "Excuse me," during a pause—and then wait for the other person to recognize you. However, interruptions *do* happen, so don't be surprised if someone finishes your sentence if you hesitate too long while you are speaking.

19. These cultures put a great deal of value on the written word. The various legal entities almost always require that contracts be written and verbal contracts are rarely legally binding. In all contracts, it's important to read the fine print, where much of the legally binding jargon is included.

20. Good topics to discuss include the local architecture, the business culture, sports (these are different in the various countries, so know the preferred sports), the arts, music, food, hobbies, nature, and history, among other things. It is best to initially avoid any topics that might be considered too personal, such as marriage status or salary.

21. The British, Canadian, and Australians eat continental style, with the fork held in the left hand and the knife in the right hand. In

the United States, the fork is held in the left hand, and the knife is held in the right hand. After cutting the food, the knife is laid down and the fork is switched to the right hand to eat the food they have cut.

The Russian, East European, and Slavic Cultures

1. A firm handshake is customary among men when meeting, departing, or meeting thereafter, whereas women may have a lighter handshake. It is considered polite to remove your gloves before shaking hands.

2. Greetings are generally reserved yet courteous, with direct eye contact and a moderate smile. Eye contact during the introduction is very important and must be maintained as long as the individual is addressing you. Once these cultures feel they can trust you as a friend, they are very warm, outgoing, and full of smiles in private.

3. Business cards are commonly used and always exchanged at meetings. The ceremony of presenting and receiving business cards is important. You can expect to participate in some form of small talk and introductory conversation before entering into business discussions.

4. Titles, rank, position, education, seniority, and the business hierarchy are important in these cultures. Although many commonly use first names, always use any appropriate titles and surnames that are cited during introductions.

5. Relationships are very important in these cultures, so be prepared to have several meetings before completing a business transaction. Show patience, because the decision-making process is slower than in the northern European countries or Western cultures.

6. It is appropriate to wait to be introduced at formal meetings. However, you may introduce yourself at an informal meeting or social gathering.

7. Business is punctual, and arriving late can make you appear to be unreliable. That being said, professional interactions also tend to be more relaxed and informal with less urgency than in the northern European countries or Western business cultures.

8. Chewing gum, whistling, slouching, leaning against things, standing with your hand in your pockets, or resting your foot on your

knee to expose the sole of your shoe are all considered rude and impolite.

9. These cultures don't initially appear to be "touching" societies. They stand about an arm's length apart until they get to know you. However, these cultures can be quite demonstrative between close friends, and physical contact is not uncommon. Hugs and embraces (like the Russian "bear hug"), cheek kissing, backslapping, and other expressive gestures are used among friends and members of the same sex.

10. First names are commonly used in business; however, if surnames (Mr., Ms., or the equivalent in their language) are used, then use the surnames until invited to use first names.

11. These cultures place a great deal of emphasis on diplomacy in newly established and more formal relationships. Once a relationship has passed through the initial phases, people feel more comfortable speaking frankly with each other and usually have less formal interactions.

12. Some of these cultures tend to be nonconfrontational and usually prefer to take an indirect approach to communication. They might replace a direct "no" with a phrase such as, "It will be difficult," or, "We will see," to maintain a certain level of politeness. That being said, there are times when they can be extremely direct and to the point; it all depends on the situation.

13. Members of these cultures are raised to be attentive listeners, so you may have to endure long periods of silence before they respond. They are careful about what they say, enjoy speaking metaphorically, and engage in considerable nonverbal communication.

14. These cultures are typically humble and modest when complimented, so being overly complimentary may make them feel uncomfortable. Avoid being perceived as self-important or, "blowing your own horn," because people might see you as egocentric or arrogant.

15. If people from these cultures lower their eyes and become silent, it is a sign that they may be uncomfortable with something you have said or done.

16. These cultures, especially Russia and Poland, generally negotiate very competently; however, some countries still have less experience with capitalism. Because they may not always fully

understand Western business practices and objectives, you may need to explain the reasoning behind some of them.

17. It is important to show the elderly in these cultures special consideration. For example, when public transportation becomes crowded, younger people are expected to give up their seats to someone older. When passing by seated people, it is polite to turn and face them and not pass with your back to them.

18. People often give gifts at the beginning of a relationship, especially when making contacts for the first time. Sometimes they are also offered at the end of a business collaboration or transaction. The best gifts are always items that are typical of or represent your culture. For instance, if you are from Switzerland, you might buy some carefully chosen chocolate. Someone from France may buy some fine French wine. Other gifts might include a book describing your country or the region you are from. If you offer flowers, check on whether it is appropriate to give even or odd numbers of them, because even numbers are associated with death in some of the countries in these cultures.

19. The OK sign and beckoning with the index finger are considered rude and obscene and should not be used in most of these cultures. To beckon someone, extend the hand palm downward and make a scratching motion.

20. The fig gesture (a clenched fist with the thumb coming through between the knuckle of the index and middle fingers) means "You won't get something" and is considered an insulting gesture throughout much of Eastern Europe.

21. Do not turn down offers of food or drink; accepting these will go a long way in developing good relationships. These cultures are very hospitable and consider it impolite to decline such offers. Dining is typically done continental style with the fork held in the left hand and the knife in the right. Before drinking, there is usually a toast "to your health" in the language of the country you are in.

The Middle East, Arabic, and North African Cultures

1. Before addressing the characteristics of the Middle Eastern cultures, let me share a word about the United Arab Emirates—because the UAE is very different from most of the other Middle Eastern cultures. I often work there, and the seven emirates (which are similar to principalities or states) are very progressive, cosmopolitan,

and clearly the most Westernized of the Middle Eastern cultures. Business styles regarding appointments, conversation, and behavior are considerably *less* traditional than in other Middle Eastern cultures. When visiting or doing business in the UAE, be sure to research the characteristics that specifically apply to them.

2. Languages of the Middle East include Arabic, Farsi, Hindi, Urdu, English, and numerous others. It's best to avoid English language acronyms and slang overall, because they might be misinterpreted and cause confusion. For example, as cited in previous chapters, the phrase *touching base* may be thought of as touching base with a jihad, because a jihad is often regarded as a base.

3. The left hand is considered the "unclean hand," so use the right hand to eat, exchange gifts, touch things, and pass food or articles.

4. Shaking hands is typical when initially meeting; however, the grip may be less firm than in some Western countries. Western men must never touch a woman or offer to shake her hand—*unless* she extends her hand first.

5. Males in these cultures are quite touch-oriented with each other, so handshakes may be prolonged and elbows may be grabbed. One of the first examples we discussed in the book was when President George W. Bush strolled hand in hand with the Saudi Crown Prince Abdullah. It's not uncommon for two men who are close friends to hold hands while walking.

6. Be prepared to exchange business cards, and be aware that it's a ritual typically done with great enthusiasm. It is important to have direct eye contact, which may sometimes be very prolonged. Avoid breaking the eye contact too often, as this may create suspicion and mistrust.

7. The basic working week is five days in the Muslim cultures, and it traditionally begins on Saturday instead of Monday. There are five daily prayers, and although prayer times vary by season, current times are usually printed in the daily newspapers. Visitors and businesspeople should be aware of the prayer times when making appointments.

8. When conversing, it is typical to stand much closer together (nose to nose) than what is common in many other cultures. Don't back away when conversing with another person, or that person will naturally lean toward you. Instead, very slightly lean toward the

other person and he or she will likely lean back somewhat. Because every culture has a natural comfort zone for how close they stand together when conversing, almost everyone will instinctively adjust to maintain that level of comfort.

9. Business tends to be more formal in these cultures than in some Western cultures. Casualness, lack of interest, insincerity, or inappropriate body language can create mistrust. It's important to have good posture, so avoid leaning on things, and keep your hands out of your pockets when conversing.

10. You must never show the soles of your shoes while sitting or standing, as this is considered a grave insult. The feet are seen as the lowest, dirtiest part of the body. It's also important never to touch anyone or point to anything with your feet. If you enter a mosque or temple, be prepared to remove your shoes and follow the appropriate protocol.

11. Time is more flexible here than in some other cultures, and things can sometimes take longer to accomplish. You'll want to show patience, because it is highly respected and appreciated. These cultures are known for fondling their "worry beads" to remind them of the virtue of patience. Avoid making anyone feeling pressured or hurried. If people from these cultures decide that they don't like you, they will simply stop listening.

12. These cultures tend to communicate less directly, so they aren't likely to openly criticize. However, they will hint or allude to changes that need to be made. They place strong emphasis on the content of a statement or written proposal, so make sure what you say and propose in writing accurately reflects your intentions.

13. Self-control is important and expected during all business transactions. Avoid showing any kind of anger; this will cause you to lose respect, which is the worst way to accomplish anything.

14. Public displays of affection between the opposite sexes are considered improper and must be avoided. Men should never stare at a woman or ask other men about their wives. However, men may indulge in enthusiastic back patting with each other in both social and business relationships.

15. Gesture "no" by tilting the head backward and either raising the eyebrows, jutting out the chin, or making a clicking sound with the tongue.

16. These cultures respect the hierarchy of structure and defer to orders from senior levels. It is important in business transactions to be very clear about communicating exactly what you expect from them. If they are unclear about what they need to do, they may take no action at all. They show great respect to their elders, as well as to those with titles and in senior positions.

17. The head is considered a sacred part of the body in the Muslim culture. Avoid touching the top of your head or face by patting, scratching, or running your hands through your hair. Never touch or pat the top of anyone's head, especially a child's. Muslim women always cover their heads when entering a mosque, and Hindu women often do the same when entering a temple.

18. Use your chin or full right hand to point, and remember that the thumbs up gesture is considered obscene. It is also impolite to point or beckon with your index finger. To beckon someone, put your hand out, palm down, and make a scratching motion with your fingers.

19. These cultures don't especially like to be in the presence of, or touched by, animals. If you invite them to your home, it's best to keep animals (especially dogs) away from them.

20. Members of the Muslim cultures usually follow strict dietary rules and do not eat pork or drink alcoholic beverages. Never give them a gift made of pigskin. In the Hindu cultures, the cow is considered a sacred animal and beef is not eaten. Never give them a gift made of cow leather.

21. Dietary habits vary greatly due to the different religious beliefs among these cultures. When dining with the various cultures, it's best to follow the "When in Rome, do as the Romans" motto— and it is *always* best to ask permission before smoking.

The Latin or Romantic Language Cultures

1. Even though the individual countries included in this category all speak a Latin-based language, it is not appropriate to refer to any of them as Latins.

2. Business hours vary widely in these cultures. They usually eat their big meal at midday, so lunch hours are generally longer than in many cultures. The midday meal is sometimes followed by a long break or siesta, as it is referred to in Spain and other

Spanish-speaking cultures. Business then resumes in the late after-noon and continues through the early evening hours.

3. It is appropriate in these cultures to greet everyone with a warm handshake, which is sometimes held longer than in other cultures. This may be accompanied by the grasping of an elbow or the touching of an arm. Men who are good friends may embrace each other with an abrazo (hug) in Spanish-speaking cultures. Depending on the country you're in, there could be one to four kisses on alternating cheeks. You should also kiss any children you meet. Kisses are given by lightly brushing cheeks together while mouthing a kiss. When departing, it's appropriate to shake every-one's hand again and follow the protocol for kissing.

4. Business cards are warmly and enthusiastically exchanged, often accompanied by expressive body language, which may include patting each other on the back in some cultures. However, in others—such as Spain—this would not be appropriate unless you were good friends. It is best to follow the cues of the country you are visiting.

5. The business approach in these cultures is initially rather formal, and fashionable business attire should be worn. However, once you've established a relationship, business may take on a less for-mal atmosphere. These cultures typically enjoy some joking and informality, so discussions can become very lively at times!

6. The use of titles is common and expected among university gradu-ates. Rank, position, seniority, and the business hierarchy are very important. Leaders are held in high regard, and these cultures also have great respect for their elders. It is appropriate to give way to elders in all public places, a habit that includes allowing them in front of you in lines and giving up your seat for them on public transportation.

7. When first meeting, and throughout the initial phases of the rela-tionship, you're apt to use titles and surnames. Although the use of first names is becoming more common when you get to know someone, always use the surnames until you are *invited* to use someone's first name. The languages of these cultures use a *for-mal* and *informal* version of the word *you*. For example, in French, the formal version is *vous*, and the informal version is *tu*. Once

you have been invited to use the informal version, the use of first names usually follows.

8. Relationships are very important, and you'll generally engage in a substantial amount of rapport building and small talk before getting down to business. These cultures tend to be warmer, more outgoing, expressive, and passionate in their communication than many others. They consider interruptions in conversation to be a sign of enthusiasm, not rudeness.

9. These cultures have demonstrative, expressive body language by many business culture standards. When working with them, it is important to be perceived as warm and responsive, rather than cool and overly stiff.

10. Punctuality varies in the Latin or romantic language cultures, especially for business social events. It is best to be punctual until you know what other people's time expectations are. Although many of the cultures have a more flexible approach to time, punctuality is important in others. For example, people in Italy and Argentina are quite punctual and will expect you to contact them if you're running late. Others, such as Spain and many Latin American countries, typically begin business meetings 15 to 30 meetings late. As discussed in previous chapters, some cultures take longer to do things. Spanish-speaking cultures might refer to this as *mañana*, meaning "not today" or "later." Patience is a virtue in these cultures.

11. Decisions usually come from the top in these cultures, so it is best to meet or negotiate with the highest level possible. There is likely to be considerable discussion before anyone makes an official decision, so be prepared for the process to take longer than it might in other cultures.

12. These cultures have abundant nonverbal language that is unique to each country. Their gestures can often communicate a message without ever using words. For example, in Italy, tapping the hand to the forehead (like a military salute in the United States) signals that "You're crazy!"

13. Certain hand gestures, including the OK sign, the Texas hook 'em horns sign, and finger pointing, are considered rude or obscene in several of these cultures and should therefore be avoided. In Italy,

the hook 'em horns gesture is known as il cornuto, which means that you are being cuckolded or your spouse is being unfaithful. In France, the OK sign is commonly used to mean "worthless" or "zero."

14. It is inappropriate to beckon someone by curling the index finger. To beckon someone, extend your hand, palm down, and make a scratching motion. To beckon a waiter, it is acceptable to use the index finger when it is pointed straight up.

15. It is considered impolite for men to stand with their hands in their pockets in public in many of these cultures. In addition, people may assume that a man standing with his hands on his hips is signaling hostility or a direct challenge.

16. Many of these cultures are Catholic, and citizens in some countries deem it inappropriate to wear shorts or sleeveless tops in churches or religious buildings. Some Catholic churches request that women cover the top of their heads with a light veil while inside.

17. Exchanging business gifts is a frequent occurrence for new business relationships in many of these cultures. However, gift giving is not typical in Brazil, so it is advisable to check the protocol for the individual countries. Gift suggestions also vary, so find out which are appropriate for the specific country you are in. In general, it is inappropriate to give white flowers, even-numbered flowers, or chrysanthemums, because they are all associated with death.

18. Music and dancing are an important part of nearly all of the Latin or romantic language cultures. As discussed in previous chapters, these cultures' languages have a great deal of melody, and the human body tends to move with the melody of one's mother tongue language. Consequently, it is not uncommon for music or dancing to be a part of business and social engagements. Many of the countries within these cultures even have dances specific to their country, such as the tango in Argentina, the samba in Brazil, or the merengue in the Dominican Republic.

19. These cultures look to embrace the philosophy of working to live, rather than living to work. The social aspect of business, and *whom* you know, is very important to them. Although business in

some cultures may be more about the know-how, it has been said that it may be more about the know *who* in these cultures.

20. When dining, meals are often accompanied by a glass of wine. Toasting is important, so learn the appropriate toast for the countries you visit. It is considered polite for a man to fill a woman's wine glass. If you don't want more wine, leave your glass fairly full and it won't be refilled.

21. These cultures generally eat continental style, with the fork held in the left hand and the knife in the right. It is appropriate to keep both hands on the table during the meal, although these cultures are tolerant of the custom of putting the left hand in your lap. People often avoid discussing business at meals and social events. They see meals as times to socialize and get to know one another; topics of conversation generally include sports, hobbies, travel, and family.

The preceding lists of cultural clues, do's, and taboos describe many of the general tendencies that these cultural categories have in common. However, they are by no means a complete list of all clues for each individual country. Remember, all of the countries within the various cultural categories mentioned have their own languages and unique characteristics; it is also advisable to do your research on the specific countries beforehand as well.

Some countries also have several distinct cultures *within* the country itself. For example, there is a strong Italian, German, British, and Spanish heritage in Argentina. This is a wide variety of cultures, so you can expect to find big differences among Argentineans' business and social styles. This holds true for many other countries around the world. As discussed in previous chapters, the business and social styles in one part of a country could be entirely different from that of another part of a country. This is exemplified by differences in the northern and southern United States, in eastern and western Canada, and among Switzerland's four distinct cultures and languages.

It is essential to learn the cultural clues, do's, and taboos, as well as the basic tendencies and expectations, of the countries and cultures you travel to and work with. For the most *successful multicultural navigation*, I suggest a review of this chapter every time your journey begins.

Win-Win Cross-Cultural Communication

The Key That Unlocks the Door to Successful Relationships

This chapter takes us full circle back to the beginning of the book. It all begins with *you* and how you start your cross-cultural relationships by being *proactive*. What do you know about another culture, and how can that help you? Do you have any preconceived ideas that may prevent you from communicating congruently and credibly? What is the best approach to take to be successful with someone from a particular culture?

It takes two to communicate, and each person involved in an exchange comes equipped with his or her own uniquely individual cultural nuances and perspectives. Cross-cultural communication is about adaptability and flexibility. People around the world are more flexible than you may think—and you can often use a sincere, honest approach to *turn resistance to assistance*. Almost everyone wants to find the comfortable middle ground of trust, rapport, and mutual understanding in their multicultural relationships.

To communicate successfully, it's important that the parties involved feel *equal* from a cultural perspective. It is very difficult to accomplish

212 Say Anything to Anyone, Anywhere

anything without a sense of shared equality. Remember, there is no right or wrong culture; they are all simply different. The surest way to damage a multicultural relationship is to make someone feel that his or her culture isn't as good as yours or that your cultural perspective is right and his or hers is wrong.

The quality of your relationships is determined by the quality of your communication. The way in which you communicate with someone from another culture determines what kind of relationship that person will want to have with you. And the degree to which you can communicate effectively will determine your degree of success in your business and social relationships.

Win-win cross-cultural communication is the *key* that unlocks the door to successful relationships. It is about avoiding the fight-or-flight syndrome so that successful multicultural relationships are possible.

The following highlights the four main categories of win-win cross-cultural communication. Only one of these categories effectively holds the key to unlock the door to successful relationships.

Win-Lose: I'm Okay—You're Not Okay

This category is a position of control for you, and one that puts the *person with whom you are communicating* in an unequal, defensive, protective, and self-defining role. It is a fight-or-flight category that forces the other person to either fight for equality, rights, position, and self-worth or to take flight and withdraw from the situation out of a sense of vulnerability and insecurity. It creates the feeling that the other person must either rebel or appease, and for obvious reasons, it clearly won't further a successful cross-cultural relationship.

Lose-Win: You're Okay—I'm Not Okay

This category also puts one party in a position of control—only this time, *you're* the one who's in an unequal, defensive, protective, and self-defining role. It too is a fight-or-flight category that compels you to fight for your equality, rights, position, and self-worth or to take flight and withdraw from the situation. This situation won't further successful cross-cultural relationships any more than the win-lose position will; the tables here are simply turned.

Lose-Lose: I'm Not Okay—You're Not Okay

This category puts everyone in a position of paralysis, where there is a complete breakdown in the communication with both parties. Because neither party is okay, it makes both feel as though they're alienated, desperate, and at the mercy of the situation. To find a way out of the paralysis requires a compromise, or some give and take on both sides' part. If both parties are willing to cooperate, this position can sometimes lead to successful collaboration by turning the lose-lose communication into win-win communication.

Win-Win: I'm Okay—You're Okay!

This is the ideal position—the one where all productive business and social communication happens. Both parties feel confident, protected, and equal from a cultural perspective. You can create rapport, establish trust, and engage in productive negotiations. There is mutual understanding, cooperation, and collaboration. It is the position where anything is possible—and it is the key to unlocking the door to successful cross-cultural relationships.

This is the end of Key Five. If you have read all five keys, you can now *say anything to anyone, anywhere,* and

Create Rapport and Organize Strategies for Success!

The Cross of Cross-Cultural

CULTURAL BLOOPERS!

The three chapters in this final section are my personal "trailer" to *Say Anything to Anyone, Anywhere*. They will certainly make you smile at the comedy of multicultural mishaps—however unintentional!

The Humorous Faux Pas

They Happen in Every Language

I've been very privileged to have had many wonderful and humorous experiences working throughout the world. I've also been fortunate not to have had too many faux pas where I unintentionally offended someone from another culture, although I've had a few! For the most part, my faux pas were more of an embarrassment to me than anyone else.

As I wrap up, I'd like to share with you a few of my stories with the most memorable international mistakes. Some of these faux pas are my own—and others I simply had the pleasure of witnessing.

When we teach our cross-cultural courses at Circles Of Excellence, we always tell our attendees to share what they have learned with their travel companions when they're heading to other countries, especially if they're going on a business trip. If you don't share what you know, you can never be quite sure about what the people travelling with you might say or do—and they'll certainly appreciate your sharing any wisdom and experience you have. I've had some firsthand experiences travelling with people that caused *my* mouth to drop!

When we were incorporating a business base of Circles Of Excellence in Dallas from Switzerland, our corporate attorney, Saul, and his wife, Bea, came to Zurich with us to handle the legalities. Bea was a tall, attractive redhead from Johnson City, Texas. She had a charming Texan accent and resembled Lucille Ball—in more than just her appearance.

As a native Texan, she prided herself on being a neighbor of former President Lyndon Baines Johnson (LBJ, as she called him). Even before we made the trip to Switzerland, I should have realized trouble was lurking when she told me the story about walking in on the former First Lady, Lady Bird Johnson, while she was seated on the commode!

When we arrived in Zurich, Bea diligently tried to pick up bits of German in order to read the road signs. The two words she picked up first were *ausfahrt* (an exit) and *einfahrt* (an entrance). Of course, her pronunciation in German—which was compounded by her Texan accent—made these words sound pretty hilarious. I'll never forget the time we were waiting for a parking space in downtown Zurich, and Bea rolled down the car window and yelled, "Would y'all hurry up and ausfahrt so we can einfahrt!" In her mind, she was simply asking them to hurry up so that we could get out of the way of other cars; however, the Swiss Germans didn't take kindly to it!

For some reason (I, of course, have my suspicions as to why) Bea really loved these two words and began to use them every chance she could. While she and Saul were staying at the Dolder Waldhaus Hotel in Zurich, she would happily let everyone know exactly when she was planning to "ausfahrt off the Dolder Bahn!" (The Dolder Bahn is the little train that takes you up the hill to the hotel.)

After Zurich, we continued on to Geneva with Saul and Bea to take care of business there. Although it might be hard to believe, Bea was actually able to top her faux pas from Zurich in Geneva. One afternoon we were having lunch at a very nice restaurant, the caliber with white tablecloths and professional waiters with white shirts and black bow ties, near the United Nations. After we were seated, one of the waiters came up to Bea and graciously asked, "Madame, would you like your water with gas or without gas?" This is a common way of asking if you want sparkling or plain water in European countries. What came next, no one could have been prepared for. Bea looked at the waiter, straight in the eye, and firmly said, "Without gas, please. I have enough gas from all this French food!" Needless to say, the waiter was appalled, and everyone at our table turned various shades of red!

In defense of Bea, I have to say that I've said some pretty silly things myself, especially in French when I first started working in Geneva. I was learning French by *submersion*—and submersed I often was. It was months before I found out that I had been calling the trash "plus belle" (most beautiful) rather than "poubelle" (the correct word for trash).

And then there was a time when I told the director's boyfriend that "She was out having her chevaux (horse) done," rather than, "She was out having her cheveux (hair) done." He looked at me ever so puzzled and replied in French, "But, she doesn't have a chevaux!" I thought that was an odd thing to say and responded, "*Of course, she does*, and she has it done every Friday at 3:00!" He began a deep belly laugh while I stood there wondering what could possibly be so funny!

That being said, my German pronunciation left more to be desired than my French. I was once returning a call to a woman whose name was "Frau Schiesse." Of course, I mispronounced the *ie* vowel in her name and called her, "Frau Sch*ei*sse." It looks like a small difference in pronunciation; however, I'm sure all of you German-speaking readers know *exactly* what I called her. And for all my non–German-speaking readers, I called her "Mrs. Shit." She promptly and *sternly* shrieked over the phone, "Frau Schiesse, Frau Schiesse, Frau Schiesse!"—*three times!* I made it a point to learn the rules on how to pronounce German vowels after that!

Fortunately, I've heard many other people make equally humorous faux pas in English. One gentleman in our Zurich office was as challenged in English as I was in German. Our company did a lot of executive coaching; however, he couldn't seem to say "executive" correctly. He always pronounced it with the accent on the *first* syllable: "*ex*-e-cutive coaching." He never could get it right—and it always sounded as though he was going to *execute* our clients! Finally, for his sake, we asked him to simply call it leadership coaching or management coaching, because it was something he could pronounce!

We had another gentleman from the office in Geneva who got big smiles when he was meeting some important people from a well-known U.S. company. He very properly shook their hands, and then said most genuinely and sincerely, "I'm very impressive!" Of course, he meant to say, "I'm very impressed." However, that wasn't quite how it was taken!

Very often I'm asked about the unusual or humorous things that occur while working with different cultures in different countries. One experience stands out beyond all others for me.

Circles Of Excellence was conducting a four-day cross-cultural training for a large international company at one of its manufacturing plants in Mexico. There was a mix of various levels of management from around the world attending. At the morning break on the fourth day, the human resources director from Europe shared his thoughts with the

U.S. human resources director and me. He told us how pleased he was with how well the training had gone, and after the compliment, he said there was just one last thing he would like to have us address in the afternoon session. We both looked at him and said we would be happy to. He then proceeded to tell us that he would like us to find a way to explain to the male employees that it was inappropriate for them to scratch their private parts in public at work! I looked at the U.S. human resources director and said, "I'm not touching that with a 10-foot pole. This one is on you!" In my business, you sometimes never quite know what you will be asked to do!

I can't end this chapter without a few words about my French husband. It's fortunate that he's such a good sport, because as a keynote speaker I frequently use examples of his language mishaps. I've talked about how he works in, "Misery" (Missouri) and often travels to "Our Kansas" (Arkansas). He accepts being affectionately referred to as Pepé Le Pew, and this faux pas of his is one of my all-time favorites.

It took place while we were dining with friends at an upscale restaurant in Dallas. We were all reminiscing and sharing stories about our school days. When it was my husband's turn, he started telling a story about how he had gotten out of a singing class in grade school due to the fact that he screamed too loud during *intercourse. The table went silent—and* we all looked at him very strangely as we tried to figure out *exactly* what he meant. The more he tried to explain—the *funnier* it became—until we finally realized that he had meant to say, "He screamed too loud during *recess.*" He had used the French words *entre cours*, meaning "between courses," as a direct translation for recess, and with his French accent it came out as—intercourse!

It makes you ask the question, "*Is* what you say what you mean?" This is always an important question to ask when you're attempting to speak another language, and you'll understand why in the next chapter.

CHAPTER
28

Is What You Say What You Mean?*

Date:	1992–11–19
Publication:	*The Wall Street Journal*
Page Number:	NA
Byline:	By Charles Goldsmith
Headline:	"Look See! Anyone Do Read This And It Will Make You Laughable"
Snippet:	BRUSSELS—Sometimes it does all get lost in translation.

*Parts of this article reprinted courtesy of Goldsmith, Charles, "Look See! Anyone Do Read This and It Will Make You Laughable," *The Wall Street Journal.*

Words Don't Always Translate the Way We Want Them To

One of the first things people realize when they communicate multi-culturally is that what we are saying may not necessarily mean what we *think* it means to other people. Throughout this book, we've discussed the fact that your words, tonality, and body language all contribute to what you say. In this chapter, we will look at what happens when the words don't always translate the way you want them to.

It's indeed humorous—but also helpful—to consider how languages and their nuances are interpreted when translating from one country to another. The following are some of the more comical translations from various languages into English.

Sometimes It Does All Get Lost in the Translation!

Attention, all travelers! A refreshingly honest airline in Copenhagen has a sign that reads, "We will take your bags and send them in all directions!" (In my opinion, *every* airline needs that sign. Wouldn't you frequent fliers agree?)

Looking for a hotel? Try one in Japan where they advertise, "You are invited to take advantage of the chambermaid." And if that isn't bad enough, there's one in Zurich that has a sign in the lobby advising, "Because of the impropriety of entertaining guests of the opposite sex in the bedroom, may we suggest that the lobby be used for this purpose." One thing is for sure: It's best to avoid the Acapulco hotel where they give new meaning to quality control. The sign in their lobby says, "The Manager has personally passed all the water served here!"

Hungry for something different? At a Polish restaurant you can select "Roasted duck let loose" or "Beef rashers beaten up in the country people's fashion." However, you may want to stay away from the Swiss restaurant with the sign that states, "Our wines leave you nothing to hope for."

Careful on elevators! A sign by one elevator in a Bucharest office building states, "The lift is being fixed for the next day. During this time we regret to tell you that you will be unbearable!"

A visit to the zoo is always a fun idea, right? Try the one in Budapest—because their zoo puts people first. Their sign says, "Please do not feed the animals. If you have any suitable food, give it to the guards on duty!"

For all you ladies who love to shop—take heed! Think twice about the Swedish furrier with the sign that says, "Fur coats made for ladies from their own skins." On the other hand, if you're looking for something a bit risqué—there's always the Paris dress shop with the sign in the window stating, "Our dresses are made for street walking." However, if you travel to Tokyo, you may want to avoid the hosiery store that advertises, "Our nylon stockings are costly, but best in the long run."

Now, for you male shoppers: Be careful to give plenty of time to the tailor on the island of Rhodes in Greece. He has a sign that warns, "Place your orders early, because in the big rush we will execute customers in strict rotation!"

But who really needs to *shop* for clothing when you can just get what you have freshened up a bit? "Drop your trousers here for best results!" suggests a Bangkok dry cleaner. And for ladies who want a little fun, there is a laundromat in Rome with a sign that reads, "Ladies, leave your clothes here and spend the afternoon having a great time!"

It's fairly common for people to dread visiting the dentist. And if you happen to be of the Protestant faith and need a tooth extraction, go to Hong Kong. The sign on the door of one of their dentists reads, "Our teeth are extracted by the latest Methodists."

But for any of you ladies who need medical attention while in Rome, be sure to stay away from the doctor with the sign that says, "Specialist in Women and other Diseases!"

Now you see why it's so important to ask yourself if *what* you say is really *what* you mean, unless of course you want to be *laughable!*

Paradoxes of the English Language

How Can a Wise Man and a Wise Guy Be Opposites?

Despite the fact that English is the "international language," there is no denying that it is also a *crazy* language. This chapter looks at the humorous paradoxes, opposite meanings, exceptions, and sometimes just plain nonsense that English frequently serves up.

There is no egg in eggplant, nor is there ham in hamburger. There is neither apple nor pine in pineapple. And while no one knows for sure what *is* in a hotdog, you can be pretty sure it isn't any kind of canine! English muffins were not invented in England, nor were French fries invented in France.

We take English for granted; however, if we explore its paradoxes, we find that quicksand works slowly and that boxing "rings" are actually square. And a guinea pig is neither from Guinea, nor is it a pig!

A lot of the same questions come to mind when we look at plurals. If the plural of tooth is teeth, why isn't the plural of booth, beeth? If you have one goose and two geese, why don't you have one moose and two meese? If there is one mouse and two mice and there is one louse and two lice, why isn't there one house and two hice?

If teachers taught, why didn't preachers praught? If a vegetarian eats vegetables, can *anyone* tell me what a humanitarian eats?

Why do people recite at a play, and play at a recital? Why do they have noses that run and feet that smell? Why do we park on driveways and drive on parkways?

Why do you get in and out of a car, but you get on and off a bus? Why do you have light when the moon is out, but you don't have light when the lights are out?

How can a slim chance and a fat chance be the same thing? How is it possible to be hot as hell one day and cold as hell the next? And how can a wise man and a wise guy be opposites?

Why is it that when a house burns up, it burns down? Why do you fill in a form by filling it out? Why does an alarm clock go off by going on?

And why, when I wind up a clock, I start it—but when I wind up this book, I end it?

Bon voyage!

ABOUT THE AUTHOR

Gayle Cotton is a National Emmy Award winner and the founder of ✍ Circles Of Excellence™ for Corporate Education. A distinguished, highly sought-after keynote speaker and executive coach, she has worked with more than 50 Fortune 500 companies. She is a faculty resource for the Young Presidents' Organization (YPO), World Presidents' Organization (WPO), Chief Executives Organization (CEO), and Entrepreneurs' Organization (EO).

While living and working in Europe, Gayle became the first American to be accepted as a member of the European Marketing and Sales Experts organization. She is a certified expert with the Executive Foundation for International Communication. She has been a TV guest on *NBC News*, *PBS*, *Good Morning America*, *PM Magazine*, *PM Northwest*, and *Pacific Report*.

Gayle has developed cross-cultural and business communication programs for the United Nations, the World Health Organization, branches of the U.S. government, and international companies on nearly every continent. After the fall of the Berlin Wall, she created video training programs to integrate the Eastern Europeans into the free market business world.

An internationally recognized authority on cross-cultural communication, Gayle educates, entertains, and inspires audiences with her fresh and unique approach. Giving new meaning to the concept of creativity and productivity, she is on the leading edge of global business communication. She offers keynote presentations on the topics of cross-cultural communication, diversity, interpersonal communication, executive leadership, presentation skills, and time management. She currently resides with her husband in Dallas, Texas.

INDEX

CPSIA information can be obtained
at www.ICGtesting.com
Printed in the USA
BVHW062306110719
553246BV00012B/114/P